a SANBORN'S book

Mexico from the Driver's Seat

Tales of the Road from
Baja to the Yucatan

By
"Mexico" Mike Nelson

Scrivener Press

a SANBORN'S book

Published by Scrivener Press in association with
Travelog & General Printing, Inc.
2009 South 10th Street
McAllen, TX 78502

Scrivener Press

P.O. Box 37175 Oak Park, MI 48237-0175

Sanborn's Logo is a registered trademark of T.G.P. Inc.
The Scrivener Press Logo is a registered trademark of
JSA Publications, Inc.

ISBN 1-878166-04-2
Library of Congress Catalog card No. 91-62784

These essays are reprinted with the permission from the
McAllen Monitor & The Mexico City News, where they first appeared.

Manufactured in the United States of America.

Photo Credit:
P. Coleman

Dedicated to Mr. Dan Sanborn, whose pioneering efforts helped millions of *gringos* (including the author's parents) to drive south of the *Rio Grande* and discover the wonderful land and people of Mexico. No man has done more for US-Mexico relations than he.

ACKNOWLEDGEMENT

There's no way to thank all the kind people who helped make this book a reality. My memory's not good enough and there's not enough room.

Special thanks go to: Craig Henderson, who opened a door, Michael Zamba, who kept it open, George Gause and Virginia Haynie, who keep better records than I do, Joe Nick Patoski, who encouraged me, Charles Nelson who put up with me, Peter Carr, who told me about ice, Lic. Gilberto Calderon Romo, Angela Corelis, Marty Hidalgo, Rolando Garcia and the Mexican Tourism Office, Gaston Rosas, and the hundreds of Sanborn's customers who wrote and gave me feedback.

Though there's no way to thank them all, thanks to the policemen, truck drivers, gas station attendants, mechanics, hoteliers, bellboys, maids and wonderful people of Mexico who have helped me in so many ways without even knowing it.

Very special thanks are due Anita Fleming for her face-saving proofreading.

Table of Contents

Don't Be Afraid of Mexico   1
The Artist's Story   3
La Pesca   5
On to Tampico   7
Tampico   9
Tampico Hotels   11
South of Tampico   13
Q & A — Part 1   15
Q & A — Part 2   17
Getting into Mexico   19
Heroism   21
Pto. Escondido   23
Pto. Angel   25
Tourism   27
Tuxpan   29
Tecolutla   31
The Day of the Dead   33
Padre Harold Miracle   35
My First in Mazatlán   37
Driving to the Copper Canyon 41
AAA   43
Pto. Vallarta   45
Try Tampico   47
Pto. Vallarta Hotels   53
Copper Canyon 2   55
Cd. Victoria   57
Cd. Victoria: Miracle   59
Prison Life   61
Durango — Mechanic   63
Huichol   65
Shortcuts   67
Dan's Story: Brothers   70
Baja Goodbye   72
Real de Catorce   75
Ghosts   78

Pto. Vallarta — Texans   81

Pto. Vallarta 84

Cd. Miguel Alemán, Tamps.   86

Tripshare   88

Gas Jockeys   90

Retirement   93

Capitalism   95

Vehicles   97

Pan American Highway   99

Dan's Story: Stuffed Grandmother   101

How to Stay Out of Hot Water   103

Itinerary — Border — Cd. Victoria — Gulf Coast 105

Mountain Kingdom   107

Itinerary — Nogales — Mazatlán — Durango 109

Ice   111

Taxi Drivers 113

Mineral Water   115

Tequila, Mezcal, & Pulque   117

Huatulco — The All-Inclusive Side   119

Huatulco — The Real People Side   121

Index   123

ABOUT THE AUTHOR

"Mexico" Mike Nelson grew up 14.5 miles from the Mexican border, near Edinburg, Texas. His parents took him on a driving trip when he was a young boy and the dust of Mexico settled on his heart. He has been going back ever since.

He remembered a striking yellow-orange, spiral-bound book from that first trip. He thought then, if he ever had to work for a living, writing that book would be great. He also had a child-like fascination with the Amazon River in South America.

He never grew up, and so was able to fulfill his two fondest childhood dreams — he went down the Amazon in a canoe in 1977 and began writing that "book with the yellow cover," *Sanborn's Travelog*, in 1987.

He's logged about a million miles on Mexican highways via car, bus, train and foot. He doesn't know everything about anything, but he knows a lot about real-life Mexico.

His musings appear regularly in a weekly column, *On the Road in Mexico* in the *Monitor*, McAllen, TX and the *News*, Mexico City. When he's not too lazy to submit them, his articles have appeared in the *Dallas Morning News*, Prentice-Hall's *RV Park And Campground Directory*, *Senior Magazine and Texas RV Magazine*. In 1991, he contributed the Gulf coast section to *Frommer's Mexico On $35 A Day*.

He has been the spokesperson for driving tourism at the *Tianguis*, the international travel & tourism convention in Acapulco, Mexico. He gave a slide presentation and seminar to journalists and travel agents in 1990.

Recognized as an expert on Mexico in the 1992 edition of *"Media Sourcebook for Experts, Authorities and Spokespersons"*, newspaper, magazine and television journalists consult him regularly.

He has several hundred slides and photos of every corner of Mexico, which he threatens to publish some day.

Don't Be Afraid of Mexico

You've probably dreamed about driving to Mexico. Now that you've got the time, you probably want to know what it's like before you jump in.

I've spent the last 20 years poking around Mexico and drive 30,000 miles a year, checking out RV parks, hotels, restaurants and out-of-the-way places.

When I'm not driving, I'm answering folks' questions or writing about what I found. You can call me at 512-686-3601, or write P.O. Box 310, McAllen, TX 78502 and I'll help you out.

Q. Do I need special insurance? What about discount insurances?

A. You must buy Mexican insurance. U.S. insurance is not recognized by the Mexican authorities. Your agent may say "Sure, you're covered," but tell it to a Mexican cop. Truth is, your policy may repair your vehicle within a few miles of the border, but it won't help you stay out of jail. Mexico operates under the Napoleonic code (like Louisiana) — you're guilty until proven innocent. No insurance, you'll go to jail until the matter is settled. Be sure the insurance you buy will repair your vehicle in the U.S. or pay you in U.S. dollars if there's a full loss. Sanborn's is one company that pays in dollars and fixes vehicles in the U.S., but if you want to shop around, there are

others. The majority do not, so ask first.

Bargains aren't always what they appear. Mexico liberalized its insurance laws this year, and companies are now free to charge whatever they want. There are more "clubs" with low rates than you can shake a stick at. Beware!

You don't have to get Sanborn's insurance to get honest service, but be careful. Only Sanborn's gives you a mile-by-smile highway guide that's good for all Mexico. A *"Travelog"* for a trip from Nogales to Mazatlan and back, for instance, contains 70 sheets of highway info (bumps, hazards, history, humor) and hotel, restaurant and RV information. There's nothing else like it.

Q. Is there unleaded gas available?

A. You bet there is. I know that a major automobile association insists there isn't, and in fact discourages folks from driving. I've driven almost everywhere in the north, west and central Mexico, and unleaded can be found. There's more every day. But you may have to plan ahead. Fill your tank whenever it reaches a quarter and you won't have a problem.

Here's a tip. If a station that has a silver pump (unleaded — "Extra") is out, they'll sometimes say that the whole town or area is out. Don't believe them. They'd rather sell you regular than have you go a mile down the road and buy from someone else who does have it. The Mexican Tourism Dept. has numbers you can call collect for any kind of information:

(91) (5) 250-0123, 250-0151, 250-8419. 250-8601, 545-4306.

The southern states — Oaxaca, Chiapas — still have a problem, but there are ways around that, too.

Diesel is available everywhere. As is regular.

Q. Safety is most people's first concern — and a good one. After all, you've worked hard to get what you've got and to have the freedom to travel the way you do.

A. I'd rather be in Mexico than any urban area of the U.S. when it comes to personal safety. Crimes against people are fewer and less violent than here.

Driving the main highways during the day is not dangerous. "Bandits" are mostly a myth. More assaults occur in U.S. rest areas and national parks than Mexican highways. Use common sense, and you've got nothing to fear.

Q. What are the roads like?

A. It depends on where you are. There's more four-lane divided highways every day. The ones that aren't are two-lane blacktop and kept in pretty good shape. As in the U.S., the richer states maintain their roads better. Most cities and towns of any size have bypasses.

Q. Is driving different in Mexico?

A. You bet it is. Like some other countries in the world, it's more free-form. Go with the flow of traffic and you'll do fine. Here are some do's and don'ts:

Never drive at night — mostly because of loose livestock and the heavy traffic.

A left turn signal isn't always the same. On a highway, it means you're giving the guy behind you permission to pass. If you want to turn left off a highway, pull over to the right, let traffic pass, then cross the highway. There are often "*retornos*" (turn-arounds) that will make it even safer. The left turn procedure is changing due to urbanization, so you can't always depend on it. Just don't put on your left blinker when somebody's behind you on a two-lane road and you'll do OK. On freeways, a left turn signal is a left turn signal.

Mexico's "Green Angels" patrol every major tourist road twice a day to help stranded tourists. Their help is free and good.

"Mexico Mike" Nelson is editor of Sanborn's Mexico News bulletin in McAllen, Texas.

Editor's note: *Extra* gas was replaced with *Magna Sin* in Nov. 1990. It is 87 octane, the same as regular unleaded in the U.S. Filling up at half a tank is prudent enough, since it is very plentiful. (Oct. 1991)

2

The Artist's Story

Climb aboard! Every week I'll carry you down a Mexican road — we'll explore the byways and meet some interesting folks who make driving the best way to truly learn about Mexico.

If, like me, you've longed to discover the "real" Mexico, you've probably skipped Tamaulipas. For years, I was impelled southward to Oaxaca, Chiapas, the Yucatan — searching for the hidden meanings of life known only by the Aztecs & Mayans. I went too far. Meaning is where you find it.

Clearing customs at Reynosa is easier than ever. The government is encouraging driving tourism, so they've simplified requirements. The *Registro Federal de Vehículos* has been absorbed by "Aduana", or customs. This means you get all your work done by one official, which speeds things up. *Mordida* is not necessary or encouraged.

Getting out of Reynosa gets my adrenalin going. Defensive driving is a way of life. "Go with the flow" is practical advice.

Hwy #97 has always symbolized freedom to me. Nothing lifts my spirits more than sailing down a good two-lane Mexican road, bounded by open land and an endless horizon. Don't sail too fast — Mexican cops have radar.

Fifteen miles south is a customs check. Now there's a red light, green light system. If you see a green light — go! You won't be delayed. Red light — stop. Neat, huh?

The next 61 miles are the longest straight stretch in all of Mexico. Scenery's pastoral and there are more cows than people.

San Fernando, 93 miles down the pike is just right for a rest stop. I got much more. That's just the way things worked out. That's Mexico — where things don't always work the way you expect, but they always work out.

Across from one of the gas stations with "Extra" (unleaded), is the Hacienda Motel. Next to that is a restaurant. Inside was a story.

Henry Kowalski is the muscular, soft-spoken, hunting guide who owns the place. Like most outdoorsmen, he was intense. He seemed a picture of serenity until he talked about hunting. His eyes burned bright and his body quivered. He's for real. If he asks, with his eyes downcast, "Do you play a little chess?", you'd better tell the truth. He's just a few points shy of holding a master rating. Like a spider, he waits for things to come to him at his little restaurant on the only road to Tampico.

"Mike, I have a story for you." Usually, I run when people say that. Not this time.

"A Mercedes pulled into my parking lot one day. Two young women, blonde and gorgeous, got out. They were twins. They unfolded a wheel-

3

chair, opened the back and lifted a man into it. He was frail-looking and white-haired. I opened the door for them."

"Naturally you are wondering about the girls. So was I. I assumed the obvious. I was envious."

The man was a paraplegic and could only move his head. He was a French painter, on his way to Mexico City. He was having a show of his works, so he must have been good. He'd always wanted to drive through Texas and Mexico, so he took the long way. He played chess with Henry.

Henry opened. The painter smiled, then told one of the twins which piece to move. She smiled too. She was his right hand. After five moves, Henry was in trouble. Four moves later, he was check-mated.

There was a kindly twinkle in the painter's smile as he told Henry he'd played the entire game in his head after they'd made two moves.

Dusk had settled. The restaurant was dark. Henry said softly, "Today, my friend, I assume very little."

The Motel Las Palmas was clean, new and quiet. I slept well. Hunting makes Henry quiver. For me it's stories. Stories like that only come from roadside cafes, comfort stops on the highway to selfdiscovery.

Next week, we'll explore a ham-mock-swinger's oasis and visit a virgin ... beachs that is!

When Mexico Mike is not on the road, he writes about it for Sanborn's Mexico Travelog, a Mexico highway guide, and con-tributes to other publications.

4

La Pesca

The new Motel Las Palmas in San Fernando, Tamps. is clean, quiet, secure. This road warrior needs a quiet place for his beauty sleep. He got it there.

Let's roll just a bit down the road today — 221 miles south of McAllen, and 118 from San Fernando. In an easy day's drive, we'll discover a "get-away" spot that won't get away with next year's budget.

Hwy #180 is fickle. Some months it's as sweet as a new girlfriend. Others, it's as mean as your boss on Monday morning. Today it's bossy. Don't let that stop you. Drive by the seat of your pants. Your posterior will tell you when to slow down. That's the secret to driving "bad" roads — slow down. Really, there's more good road than bad. Sadly, it's easier to remember the bad about roads or people.

160 miles south of McAllen, like a desert mirage, a small mountain range — the Rusias — materializes. Abruptly, the road slices through the bellies of white limestone hills. A few villages appear like magic kingdoms, then disappear so quickly that you wonder if you imagined them.

Soto la Marina is 81.5 miles south of San Fernando. We'll turn right at the crossroads and meander 37 miles to La Pesca, sliding through more mountains to the Gulf. It's an hour and a half from San Fernando.

La Pesca is rich in contrasts. The very rich and the very basic enjoy it side-by-side. The **Campo La Pesca** is fancy. It sports an elegant reception hall, well-kept grounds and several cabanas. They're Mediterranean style: beds on pedestals, ceiling fans, gauze curtains and air-conditioning. The staff will take you hunting or fishing, clean your catch or dress your kill, then cook it for you. All you have to do is enjoy yourself. It's reasonably priced for what you get. Satisfied clients include ex-governors, C&W stars & just plain rich folks. You'll be treated like royalty. It's run by Claudio "Cavi" del Río and his mother. "Cavi" is in McAllen much of the time. Call him at 632-6849.

A hundred yards east is the **Motel Villa del Mar**. It's as humble as the Campo is elegant. The eight rooms are spotless and there's space for six self-contained RV's. In a grassy area stands a palm-thatched palapa, facing the Río Soto la Marina.

"I built that" the owner said with pride. "People come here to get away from their troubles. Listening to the water helps them, so I built this shrine to serenity. God was kind to me and this place, so I gave back what I could." If you don't have a hammock, he'll scare one up for you.

You can sit on the pier that jut into the river, with your feet dangling in the warm, brown water. He built that with his own hands, too. He's a simple, humble man who makes the best with what he's got. He'll make

5

you feel like one of the family. He'll never be rich, but he's certainly not poor in the things that count.

The river runs into the Laguna Madre Sur, a few miles east. The beach is okay and undeveloped. You can buy fish from the boats. They're so fresh they flop. It's crawling with crabs and oysters, too.

An Old Gringo lives in the motel. He says this was the only cheap hotel with hot water. He's tried them all. You see him everywhere, this Old Gringo. He's retired, drives a beat-up Ford, divides his empty time between La Pesca (or San Blas or some other out-of-favor beach) and Houston (or Chicago or Ames). He's always alone; always had a wife who died or just gave up.

He wears baggy shorts, motions with age-spotted hands and has alcohol-sour breath. This one wore lots of gold jewelry, but not enough to hide the liver spots that shouted his life story. He'd sown a bitter crop in his youth. Now he's harvesting its fruit. He likes La Pesca. The hotel owner looks after him. That is his family.

Mexicans are compassionate people. They don't understand families that don't take care of their elderly. They know that kindness is free, but it is not cheap. Even the poorest of them showers *amistad* (friendship) on those who can get it nowhere else.

Mexico's full of expatriates of all ages. Attracted by the beauty of the land; they stay, entranced by the graciousness of her people. Many have gone there seeking only peace and found healing. I did, once. Maybe the Old Gringos, will too. When you meet one of these *viejitos* (oldsters), talk to them. Listen. That's all they ask.

Next week we'll try Tampico, where we'll eat at a restaurant that looks like a Jack London hangout. Later we'll watch the "Birdman of Tampico" as he wages a lonely battle against park pigeons. Meanwhile, I'll just put up my hammock and snooze.

When "Mexico Mike" isn't snoozing, he's driving the highways of Mexico keeping Sanborn's Travelog updated, or contributing to various publications.

On to Tampico

Sunday, July 8, 1990

I hope everyone enjoyed swinging in La Pesca! Three hours (131 miles) more and we'll be in Tampico — unless we stop and fish along the way. I just heard they're biting at Española!

Enjoy the rocky, hilly, scenery after you turn south from Soto la Marina. Hilly stands of gumbo limbo and "ghost" (cottonwood) trees are nice on the eyes for the next 60 miles. Then it'll be flat halfway through Veracruz state.

Fishermen, you're in luck! Lavaderos, 23.5 miles south can be a hot spot, but right now the water's pretty low. Don't despair. Presa República Española, 15 miles down #180 and two miles west is another story.

According to James Mayo, who runs fishing/hunting groups out of Monroe, La, (318-323-8612) the fish are hotter than the McAllen weather.

His people say black bass are begging to be liberated. His groups **released** 60 bass from 5-8 pounds because they felt sorry for them. They kept the 8-10 pounders. The last group took 148 sacks of fish. A sack, they told me, is about the size of a plastic lunch sack.

He's got a camp there, which he bought from Steve Murray, a San Benito outfitter who run's "Trips Unlimited".

I met Steve once and he seemed to be a down-to-earth outdoorsman who really loves Mexico. You can't be much higher in my book.

Steve has a really nice lodge on Lavaderos with central air, microwaves, ice-makers etc. It sleeps 12, and he has fishing packages for $590 for 4 days, 3 nights. This includes everything —food, lodging, fishing, etc. Call Steve at (512) 399-8800.

He'll get you to the fishing. He's got a good idea — mobile units ready to roll where the fishing or hunting is, if it's not at his ranch.

One of those fine folks will help you have a good time, and maybe catch some fish. I promise to stay away, so that my famous ill-luck doesn't jinx the spot. Of course in fishing, ain't no guarantee.

The road between the two towns, is very literary. First, you'll cross the Tropic of Cancer; then Rancho Moby.

The hills disappear as suddenly as they arose and you flatland it into Tampico. About 30 miles north, you pass a Pemex with "Extra" (unleaded) and lady attendants in flaming orange jumpsuits. Don't worry, they're just bright, not lit. One of them told me her boss prefers women employees because they're more courteous and honest than men.

Just before Altamira the road divides and the pace of traffic picks up. The controlled anarchy that is driving in Mexican cities takes over.

7

If you let it take you over, allow yourself to flow with the traffic, you'll learn to love it. If you don't, it'll beat you down.

RV'ers — the only park in Tampico is at mile 126.6 of your *Travelog*, on the right. **Muralta's** is on a golf course and lake has all hookups and is one of the prettiest I've seen.

Tampico was the beginning setting for *The Treasure of the Sierra Madre,* by the way. It was also the site of the Mexico's first regular air service, which went to Mexico City, with oil companies payrolls.

One of my favorite things to do in Mexico is to hang around the plaza. Whole families still turn out to stroll, relax and people-watch. Here, I like the Plaza de Armas about sunset. The blackbirds prefer it too, filling the trees with their boisterous selves. They, in turn, attract the "bird man of Tampico".

He's a proud, white-haired, mustachioed living scarecrow, between 60 and 90 years old.

Funereally clad in a black coat, pants, hat, sporting a thick multi-colored wooden cane, he'll chat with you about anything. He always smiles — until a nearby tree fills with birds. Then he'll dash off, slam his cane into the tree, **WHAP, WHAP,** 'till they fly, screeching, away. He'll shake his fist, turn triumphantly and start chattering to a tree, or a person nearby. We talked, but I didn't find out why he hates the birds so. Of course, he's not alone in that, is he?

Mexicans are more tolerant of their crazies than we are. So long as they aren't harming anyone, they let them be. We could learn a lesson from them.

Next week we'll visit each of the main hotels here and a few of the restaurants. You'll be surprised — I was.

If you'd like to take a driving trip, but can't find anyone to go with you, here's an idea! A free service called "Tripshare" links drivers with riders (or those who want to caravan). It works like a college ride-board. Send your name, a mailing address (preferably a P.O. Box), where, how and when you want to go, to TRIPSHARE, P.O. Box 310, McAllen, TX 78502. Please specify who you won't go with (smokers, opposite sex, etc.). A copy of the list will be sent to everyone on it. Find somebody going when you are and work it out!

"Mexico Mike" updates Sanborn's Mexico Insurance Travelog in Mc-Allen when he's not telling fish stories.

8

Tampico

Sunday, July 15, 1990

Try Tampico! Only six hours south of McAllen or Brownsville sits a small city as lively as Veracruz, as seedy as any seaport, and incongruously guarding a virgin — beach, that is.

Dismissed as "Mexico's Houston" by most guidebooks, few tourists spend time here. They hurry-scurry southward in search of the very thing they missed in Tampico. I know: I was once one of them.

Eating's my second favorite thing to do in Mexico. One of the neatest and cheapest treats is the lowly *liquado* — a Mexican smoothie. The best ones come from open-air stands, not restaurants.

The *liquadero* (you can add "ero" to almost any word to mean the guy who does it, "era" for gals) stuffs papaya, melon, guayaba, banana, ... into a blender, adds cinnamon, milk, sugar or honey. You can ask for wheat germ, yogurt, eggs, nuts, granola or ...

A few *"whirrrrl's"* later he'll pour a frothy brew into a styrofoam cup. Plunk a straw into it and suck away! It may be the best deal in Mexico.

While Tampico's not a gastronomical mecca, there's good, honest food. I'm no gourmet, though I do like snails and know what a fish knife is for.

My favorite seafood haunts are neighbors. Finding two unique restaurants on a main plaza that aren't ticky-tacky rates high in my book.

Diligencias is the winner, due to its huge portions. If you're hungry, go there. Take about $20 for two. Sr. Miguel Angel Castillo, of the Tourism Dept. told me of it. We both owe him one. They had, perhaps, the best seafood I've ever had.

The outside might put you off, since it's plain and the neighborhood borders on seedy, but be brave. The best things in Mexico are always beneath the surface.

The inner dining room is a "white-tablecloth" sort of place. You can order from over 100 dishes. If you get the appetizer, *Fiesta de Siete Mars*, don't order anything else. The sad-eyed, white-coated waiter tried to tell me, but I was too smart. Don't you be.

Saloon Palacio is the sort of place I imagine Jack London haunted. Sailors have rolled in and out of here for years. It's been cleaned up, but the atmosphere of transient decadence is still there, lingering like an exotic musk.

Salt-soaked sea chests are stored in the rafters, forgotten testaments to men probably dead. The floor and some tables, are marble. The bar has a brass rail, but no stools.

A marvelously voluptuous, hard-used mermaid who used to split the waves leers at you from the corner. **Careful!** You'll pass dangerously close to her when you go to the bathroom.

Their menu's not as ambitious as its neighbor, but they do offer good *huachinango* (red snapper) stuffed with shrimp and crab. They also have steaks for meat lovers. The price is about the same.

Away from the dock a few blocks is the **Cafe Mundo**, at the corner of Miren and Lara. It is not *El Mundo* (the world) simply *Mundo*. It's the "city diner" of yesteryear. Open 24 hours, it feeds students, office workers and old-timers who look like they may be planning a new Revolution.

The tables wobble. The tablecloths don't match. The windows don't get cleaned very often. The same three waiters seem to be there all hours, which may be why they look like ushers at funeral parlors. It's my kind of place.

The food's good and cheap. Coffee's hot and black. Breakfast costs $3-4 for two, lunch $4-6, dinner $4-8. I had the best bacon there. Generally, in Mexico, bacon and eggs are cooked together. Here, it was thick slices, dark and crisp, *al lado* (on the side).

The **Gran Muralla China** has two locations that are a world apart. The one downtown is simple and good. The one by the Posada Tampico charges extra for rice. I asked the owner and he said it was the Mexican way. I thought Chinese food was the same the world over. I was wrong.

La Mansión across from the Camino Real is an elegant, old mansion decorated in French Provincial style. It'll cost a couple $40 or more for dinner.

Recent news: the narcotics **roadblocks** on the highways were **eliminated** this week.

Steve Walker's taking some kindred souls on a camping trip to Potosi the 27th — 29th. Call him at 548-1384.

Next week we'll sleep around town and visit that virgin I've been telling you about. The beach, I mean.

$$$$$$$$$$$$$$$$$$$$$$$$

When not eating, "Mexico Mike" drives Mexico updating the highway guide, Sanborn's Travelog, for Sanborn's Mexico Insurance.

Tampico Hotels

Sunday, July 22, 1990

Now that you're well fed, let's go to bed! Tampico hotel prices vary according to the day of the week. On weekends, even I think about reservations.

One of the landmarks of the city is a green, curved glass building with many windows on the edge of the waterfront.

It's called *edificio de la luz* (building of light) because it was one of the first buildings with electric lights. They were so bright that they lighted the streets all around.

Today it's a seaman's hotel where the ghosts of sailors who died in agony roam its dank, dark halls. Their pathos soaked into the walls.

The fanciest (and highest-priced) hotels are on Hidalgo, a busy street that runs north-south on the west edge of town.

The first you'll see is the **Posada de Tampico**. Its 140 rooms are big, comfortable and quiet. It has tubs. The grounds are tropical. They're always constructing more rooms, so check out the location of yours, or you might be awakened by nail-pounding early in the A.M.

They have a pool, parking, putting green, kennel, a gourmet restaurant, and a nightclub. It's far enough away from the rooms that it won't disturb sleepers. Cost for two is between $60-75. PH: (12) 28-0515, 28-0575.

Down the street, in every way, is the **San Antonio Courts**. It's a three story "U-shaped" affair with 90 rooms that vary from pretty bad to OK. I have to be honest. One night, I needed a room and they gave me one that, well ..., I've seen better. PH: (12) 13-0165.

This roadlogger was steamed, and was ready to scrape the "OK SANBORN'S" sticker off their window. Fortunately, a cooler head prevailed.

The next day I talked to a fellow who lived there. He explained that the higher you go, the better they get. It's convenient, but check out the room before you check in.

The Grand Dame of Tampico hotels is the **Inglaterra**. It's a downtown landmark across from the main plaza. It's old-fashioned and quality. Its 126 rooms are ok and most have tubs. It has an elegant restaurant and parking. They have a bar with live music, but the managers assured me it wouldn't be disco. Let me know.

Costs fluctuate like my blood pressure. The rack rate was $60, but it depends on the season. If business is slow, you can get great bargains. Ask. Ph: (12) 12-5678.

The **Posada del Rey** is the oldest hotel in town, but has been remodeled. The staff was friendly and its 60 rooms are OK. The inside ones seemed to be quiet. You can park across the street at the Blanco lot. Rooms cost about $30. PH: (12) 14-1024, 14-1331.

The **Impala** is a bargain! It's 4 stories house 80 rooms that are different sizes, but all adequate. It's not fancy, but it's nice. It has an elevator and a drive-in garage. As a **Sanborn's Club** member, you will receive a 20% discount. Otherwise, it'll cost between $35-45. PH: (12) 12-0990, 12-0684.

The **Monte Carlo** is an OK place, but the management is not. Rooms are small; some are noisy. Their elevator makes the weirdest sound, which is interesting. If your room is close to it, it's deafening. The small restaurant is cozy, though pricey. Rooms cost $40-55. PH: (12) 14-1093.

The **Suites Princess** is a bed and breakfast place at Ave. Ayuntamiento and E. Nacional. They have a kitchen and you can cook your own or ask the owner to do it for you.

The charming 8 rooms are pleasant and homey. It'd be good for long-term visits. Be aware, though, that it's sandwiched between a disco called Paradise and an organ bar name Sioux!

My favorite is the **Tampico**, at Carranza #513 Ote. It's away from the square, but downtown. It's an "Ex-Grand Hotel". It's only been operating since Dan Sanborn, but it looks older. Staff was friendly. It has three stories wound around a ballroom that bespeaks of faded elegance. It's sometimes used for private parties, so ask. The aquarium in the lobby was clean and the fish looked as happy as fish can.

Cost is about $22-28. PH: (12) 12-4970.

The virgin I told you about is the beach. Just follow the blue "tourist route" signs with a palm tree and waves through the Pemex plant.

The road dead-ends into a white-sand beach that looks like Padre did before condomania struck. There are miles of sands, dunes and no buildings!

There's one restaurant on a hill and several mom and pop eateries on the road. It won't last long, though. My Tourism guide proudly assured me that there was a project afoot to turn this into "another Cancun".

I tried to explain to her that that would ruin it and some of us gringos appreciate the "other" Mexico. She was young and polite and didn't understand. I drove back to town feeling old and sad. That's progress.

$$$$$$$$$$$$$$$$$$$$$$$$$

When not being sad, "Mexico" Mike hits the road updating the highway guide, Sanborn's Travelog for Sanborn's Mexico Insurance.

South of Tampico

Sunday, July 29, 1990

As much fun as it was, it's time to leave Tampico.

There are two ways out of town, heading south. One is over the unique bridge that dominates the skyline. Spain gave Tampico an award for building such an artistic way to cross a river.

The other one heads west, towards Valles, then turns south the other side of the *Laguna de Chairel*, after crossing the *Río Panuco*. Sadly, it also passes the dump, so you might want to pass it up.

The bridge is fairly new — about two years old. Old-timers will wax obscene about the ferries that used to hinder your escape from Tampico.

They operated on a schedule that changed like (or with) the tides by rules that weren't even that consistent.

Sometimes one took passenger cars, sometimes the other. A bridge was under construction for years and hung half-done, mocking those who ferried under it.

Every winter, hordes of gringos descend on the Gulf coast. Many asked me with a mixture of hope and resentment about the process of "The Bridge". If you were Gulf-bound, there was no other.

Today this toll bridge will save you several hours over the dump road. Besides, the view is great, and the smell is nicer.

You'll see the *Río Panuco* running swiftly below you, Tampico spread behind you and the Gulf way off to the left. The *Panuco* is so big that many folks imagine it to be the Gulf. Now that you know, you can correct anyone in your car who makes that mistake. Go ahead — feel superior.

Once across, you're in the state of Veracruz. Divided highway peters out after a few miles and the infamous Hwy #180 returns.

Veracruz is a rich state, one of the richest in Mexico. Until recently, this highway has not reflected that. With the federal government's emphasis on surface tourism, that's changed. Not one person has come into my office recently saying bad words about the highway between Tampico and Veracruz.

You'll pass a gas station with *Extra* just after you cross. Then, in season, (May — June), you'll see folks selling pineapples from stands along the road. For me, this's one of the things that makes Mexico a pleasure. I like stopping at a little stand where a family is selling fruit, coconuts, honey or who-knows-what.

Whatever you buy there was probably produced by the person selling it (or his family). The money you leave behind goes directly into the local economy. International corporations are fine; nice hotels are fine, too; but the feeling I get from helping a little guy make an honest peso can't be beat.

People are different and there are many Mexicos. There's one for each of us. You'll never find yours unless you hit the road and let it find you.

I sent a German down this road who didn't enjoy his trip. The only pleasant words he had about it came from the interactions he had when he stopped at some of these stands and others farther south.

Years from now this will be his memory of Mexico. He spoke no Spanish, but he communicated. So will you. There's no guarantee you'll enjoy every minute of your trip, but by trying some of these unique things along the way, you better your odds.

After 40 miles, you'll pass the little town of Ozuluma, two kilometers off the road. Col. Francisco Mascarenas fought the forces of the ill-fated French usurper, Maximilian there. Maybe it's because of the unsettled ghost-soldiers who died there, but the road is sometimes pretty bad in here.

Lately, it's been ok. My notes say the potholes are "sneaky". Wonder what that means?

You'll skirt the town of *Naranjos* (oranges), but hold onto your britches. How did a restaurant called "Mr. Ed's" get out here?

A roadlogger's a curious beast, so I went back. The owner was friendly and speaks English. He'd spent several years in the U.S., and had come home.

The place was spotless and his family industrious. They have good *enchiladas* and seafood. The steaks, he assured me, were a cut above anyone else's in town, but I didn't try one.

Since the TV show by the same name had helped him learn English, he thought the name would bring good luck. I hope it does.

There's a whole generation of Mexicans who came to the U.S. as illegals and have gone home. They are the nucleus of a new nation — bilingual, appreciative of both things Mexican and U.S., and enterprising.

Many of us are "going home" now. We reach an age when it's just the right thing to do. Universal truths like that cross boundaries of nations and languages.

$$SSSSSSSSSSSSSSSSSSSSSS$$

Now that he's home, "Mexico Mike" spends most of his time "going away" updating Sanborn's Travelog for Sanborn's Mexico Insurance in McAllen.

Q & A — Part 1

Sunday, August 12, 1990

Folks, I've gotten a lot of requests for more practical information about driving to Mexico, so I'm going to give you the best answers I have on the most common questions I get.

I've spent the last 20 years poking around Mexico and drive 30,000 miles each year, checking out RV parks, hotels, restaurants and out-of-the-way-places. I decided I needed to do this after nearly getting into a fight with a lady at church who told me it was unsafe to drive in Mexico. Since I'm a better writer than fighter, I figured this was the prudent course of action.

MYTH: "Pothole ridden", a driver complained of the roads after a trip to a rural area. "I wouldn't even ride a burro on some of those roads."

REALITY: True, there are potholes on certain roads, which is a situation that occurs in every country. Major roads however, tend to be in decent shape and are easy to navigate. Be safe and confine your driving to the daylight hours. You can't see potholes at night. I consider myself an expert pothole-dodger (in fact I get a kick out of it when successful — a jolt when not) and even I miss 'em in the dark. Please note, if you are riding a burro, the road always feels like it has potholes.

MYTH: Mexico is unsafe.

REALITY: This is most peoples' first concern — and I'll give you a straight answer. What really bugs me is folks who don't drive who bad mouth driving in Mexico. I guess I just don't understand people who have closed minds and won't listen to the facts. But most people who ask me sincerely want to know, so I keep trying. I'd rather be in Mexico than any urban area of the U.S. when it comes to personal safety. Crimes against people are fewer and less violent than here. On the whole, Mexico is safe to visit. As for highways, local, state and federal officials patrol the routes constantly. An emergency road service program called the Green Angels, which is run by the Ministry of Tourism helps travelers who have automobile troubles. Driving the main highways poses no threat to anyone. Bandits are more myth than reality. They no more rule the Mexican highways than Hell's Angels rule the California freeways. More assaults occur in U.S. rest areas and national parks than Mexican highways. Use common sense and you've got nothing to fear. Now I have some local friends who are arrowhead hunters. They go out 'way off the beaten track. There are some areas where it's risky to do that and some that aren't. Steve Walker takes campers into the high country all year and it's perfectly safe.

I know that you've heard someone talk about an "incident" that happened to someone they "heard of", but didn't actually know and weren't really sure when it was..... Most of those stories happened a

15

long time ago or involved people
who were more than tourists (mis-
sionaries, DEA agents, drug deal-
ers, family of local folks who were
having a feud, etc.). I still hear peo-
ple talk about the incidents in Gua-
dalajara that occurred 10 years ago
as if it was yesterday. Enjoy your-
self and be a tourist. Most people
are friendly and helpful. TRY IT
BEFORE YOU KNOCK IT!! See-
ing Mexico by land offers a unique
perspective on the country and its
people. This will provide an oppor-
tunity to see Mexico on the ground.
Give it a try.

Q & A — Part 2

This is a continuation of last week's realities and myths about driving. We had a report that "Mex", as his friends call him, is lost in the wilds of Chiapas, but we know that a Travelogger never gets lost — just misplaced. He claims to have a great story for us, but we think he's just making it up. He thinks he saw the ghost of B. Traven or something.

MYTH: My car will be stolen the moment I cross the border. A fellow who recently came here from the North (north of Red Gate), actually told me he was going to park his car at the mall and rent a car to drive to Monterrey because he was afraid it would get stolen.

REALITY: Insurance company losses are less than for U.S. companies. You've got a better chance of having your vehicle stolen at home than in Mexico. RV thefts are negligible.

Q: What are the roads like?

A: It depends on where you are. There's more 4-lane divided highway every day. The ones that aren't, are two lane black-top and kept in pretty good shape. Like in the U.S., the richer states maintain their roads better. Most cities and towns of any size have bypasses.

Q: Is driving different in Mexico?

A: You bet it is! Like some other countries in the world, it's more free-form. Go with the flow of traffic and you'll do fine. Here are some do's & don'ts:

1. Never drive at night — mostly because of loose livestock and the heavy traffic.

2. A left turn signal isn't always the same. On a highway, it means you're giving the guy behind you permission to pass. If you want to turn left off a highway, pull over to the right, let traffic pass, then cross the highway. There are often retornos (turnaround) that will make it even safer. The left turn procedure is changing due to urbanization, so you can't always depend on it. Just don't YOU put on your left blinker when somebody's behind you on a two-lane road and you'll do okay. On freeways, a left turn signal is a left turn signal.

3. Mexico's Green Angels patrol every major tourist road twice a day to help stranded tourists. Their help is free and good.

4. Please buy MEXICAN insurance. U.S. insurance is not recognized by the Mexican authorities. Your agent may say — Sure, you're covered for so many miles, but tell it to a Mexican cop. Mexico operates under the Napoleonic Code (like Louisiana) — you're guilty until proven innocent. No insurance, you'll go to jail until the matter is settled. I know. I did once, because I was too "smart" to get Mexican insurance. That was when I was younger and handsomer.

Q. Is unleaded gas available?

A. You bet there is! I've driven

17

most everywhere in the North, West and Central Mexico and unleaded can be found. Here's a tip. If a station that has a silver pump (unleaded — Extra) is out, they'll sometimes say that the whole town or area is out. Don't you believe them! They'd rather sell you regular than have you go a mile down the road and buy from someone else who does have it! The Mexican Tourism Dept. has numbers you can call collect for any kind of information: (91) (5) 250-0123, 250-0589, 250-0151, 250-8419, 250-8601, and 545-4306.

The southern states — Oaxaca, Chiapas — Still have a problem, but there are ways around that, too. In fact, a local customer came back just last week and gave me a list of stations in Oaxaca and Chiapas. I'll be checking it out myself soon. Last week a local couple came back and thanked me for a wonderful vacation. I suggested they go to those southern states and they loved it. They said they found unleaded everywhere (though they had to look hard sometimes), except in Tampico on the way back. It was a weekend and the station they stopped at was out. There may have been others, but they just bought some "Nova" (leaded) and came home. Diesel is available everywhere, as is regular.

"Mexico Mike" now tells us he has not seen B. Traven's ghost. He says he is B. Traven. We think he's gone into the heart of darkness, so we've sent a patrol to find him.

Getting into Mexico

Sunday, August 26, 1990

More folks worry about **how** they're going to get into Mexico than **what** they're going to get out of a Mexican adventure. **RELAX!** It's easy as pie and smooth as silk. Mexican *"aduana"* (customs) officials are human and usually reasonable.

PROVE you own your rig with your original (or notarized copy) of your title. If it's "owned" by the bank, you should have a notarized letter authorizing you to take it to Mexico. If you're taking someone else's rig, then you **have** to have a notarized permission from the owner. This is enforced.

ONLY ONE VEHICLE to a customer, so if the car or motorcycle is in the same name as the rig, assign permission to drive it to someone else (husband, wife, "other"), via a notarized statement. If your Mexican insurance broker is any good, he'll have a notary at his border office. Remember — the holder of the permit must be in the vehicle any time it's being driven. He doesn't have to drive, just be a part of the upholstery.

DEMONSTRATE financial responsibility. Mexican law does not recognize "foreign" (American, Canadian, other) insurance. Have an accident without insurance written by a Mexican company, and you **WILL GO TO JAIL.** You'll get out when the other party is satisfied that you've paid for their damages. I did once, and it wasn't my idea of a vacation.

CITIZENSHIP. Everybody has one, but customs officials worldwide are a suspicious bunch. Passport, birth certificate (or notarized copy), voter's registration coupled with a picture ID will do. Your insurance agent may notarize an affidavit of citizenship if you don't have any of the above and don't look too shady. You'll get a Tourist card at the border.

KIDS. Minors must have the same stuff as adults. If only one parent's travelling (even if they're split up) you'll need a notarized letter of permission or proof of sole custody. Getting back to the U.S. can be tough with a child. I'd have a picture of both taken by a photographer in the U.S. and have it notarized. I'm serious. This is seldom a problem, but when it is, it's a big one.

STUFF. This includes **food**, drugs, **booze**, smokes, **cameras, video equipment, tv's etc.** Don't worry. A reasonable amount of anything for personal use is acceptable. One TV, ok, Ten TV's, no.

COMPUTERS. This is changing, so check with the Mexican consulate before you go.

CB'S. Officially, you must register them in Mexico City, but it's not enforced.

HAM RADIOS. A bit trickier, but so are hams. Register them with the nearest regional Delegación Regio-

19

nal de Concesiones y Permisos de Telecomunicaciones. There are 14 of them. This is enforced, but the permit's readily granted. Request info from *Liga Mexicana de Radio Experimentadores (LIMRE)*, APDO 907, 06000, Mexico, D.F. PH: (011-52-5) 563-1405, 563-2264.

PETS. Show a certificate of good health, up-to-date shots and Bowser or Puddy'll cross with you. Officially, you're supposed to take him to a Mexican vet and get a letter from him, but this is rarely enforced.

GUNS. Unless you're hunting — NO! NO! NO! Get the picture? Hunters, your outfitter will handle permits. You'll need to bring your own gun. If you're not hunting, you don't need a gun. **ALWAYS ENFORCED — EVERYWHERE IN MEXICO.**

FINALLY — if you run into an official who's had a bad day, remember you don't have to pay anything. The Mexican government is really trying to cut out the old ways. If an official refuses to let you cross, remember, he has a supervisor, and there are several border crossings. Pen in hand, ask his name and badge number. Tell him you're calling "*Contraloria*". A nationwide toll free number is: 91-800-00-148. Ask to see his "*jefe*" (boss).

A Mexican adventure can be the most rewarding, or most frustrating, time of your life. It all depends on your attitude. Take each day as a new one and it'll work out. There's a saying, "In Mexico, there is always a way." Note that is doesn't say **your** way (or mine).

"Mexico Mike" is on the road to Oaxaca & Chiapas supposedly updating the Travelog, but we think he's goofing off.

20

Heroism

Sunday, September 2, 1990

Heroism is something you carry inside you. You never know when you'll need it.

A local fellow, Eric Contreras, unpacked his on the road between Oaxaca and Pto. Angel, recently.

We were in Oaxaca with the Inter-American Council, which promotes McAllen businesses in Mexico. The only commercial interest I have is what's on sale at the mall, but they let me tag along anyway.

I left early to do what I do best — inspect hotel beds — with Michael Zamba, a writer from Mexico City. He'd just finished a book soon to be published by Sanborn's, *Mexico by Land — The Colonial Heart*. He thought travelling with me would be a vacation!

We drove Hwy #175 to Pto. Angel. It may be the least popular road in Mexico. If it was an animal, it would be a snake intent on ingesting its tail. It doesn't have rest stops — it has upchuck pullouts. A mere 147.8 miles from Oaxaca to Pochutla takes 6 hours!

The good news is there was unleaded gas on the way and at Pochutla. 89 miles out of Oaxaca is the "Hotel 6", a 400 year-old ex-hacienda. I heard it was once a lesbian-vegetarian commune, but I didn't see any veggies, so I guess it changed hands.

A crew was painting white stripes down the middle of the road. I joked it would be a shame if a rockslide ruined their work.

Eric showed up in Pto. Escondido a day late. He'd bussed from Oaxaca. About halfway, the driver got intimidated by some small rock slides on the road. The passengers insisted he push on.

After the point of no return, the highway was completely covered with rocks, dirt and boulders. "Even a Texan couldn't get through that," Eric admitted.

The driver wanted to turn back. Our boy said, "I learned that when you can't go around something, you go over or through. Looks like it's over."

He's persuasive, that lad. He's also 6'2" and muscular. He convinced the driver to call Pochutla and arrange for a bus to meet them on the other side of the slide.

The passengers were a mixed lot. There was Dr. Barry Keller, of Santa Barbara, CA, a 50 year-old hydrogeophysicist/surfer who loves big waves and volcanoes. Accompanying him were a surfboard, a wife Rosie, and a 19 year-old daughter, Daphne. She was between semesters at Harvard.

Manuel Escobedo was in his 60's and had been born in Pto. Escondido. His wife, daughter and four day old granddaughter were with him. 31 regular folks and a French couple rounded out the lot.

The slide was big. The mess completely covered about two hundred yards of road. Two football fields are more intimidating when they separate you from certain death if you miss a step.

From the road to the floor of the canyon below was maybe a thousand feet.

Eric admitted, "Things were a little tense. The slide was fresh and loose. We didn't know if there would be others. Every step we took sent small avalanches rolling to the canyon floor."

A LITTLE TENSE?

Eric's a strong fellow (and apparently sure-footed — in fact, his friends say he has many goat-like qualities at times). He was one of the first to cross the slide with his bags. That's no story.

He then re-crossed the treacherous mess to help those who might have trouble — like the mother of the four day-old baby.

She couldn't make it with her luggage and the baby. Her 60 year-old grandfather couldn't help. She was hysterical. Eric calmed her down and took care of them. He made sure the whole family got across. That's part of a story. He crossed the slide "several times" to encourage people and help them.

Finally, he crossed with Dr. Barry's surfboard. **That's** a story. Picture a six foot, two inch Texan, topped by his ever-present white cowboy hat, carrying a surfboard across a rockslide in the Oaxacan pine forest at 5800 feet — as night falls. Above is the timber line. Below is a thousand foot drop.

"Why'd you do it," I asked.

"Somebody had to. When people need help you do what you can. We all bonded there in the mountains. Heck, I just carried little stuff. Besides," he grinned shyly, "it was kind of fun. I think there are three kinds of people: the ones who make things happen, the ones who watch things happen and the ones who wonder what happened. I just know which one I am."

Later, we saw the French couple on the street. They didn't recognize Eric. He reminded them. They smiled politely. I was going to call the office and issue an advisory, but as I dialed, a bus roared through.

The road was clear. Fame and road closures are fleeting in Oaxaca.

$$\text{\$}$$

"Mexico Mike" updates Sanborn's Mexico Travelog to justify his wandering. but we think he's a spy.

Pto. Escondido

Pto. Escondido, Oaxaca is a hotbed of emotion. Anyone who's been there feels passionately about it.

The smart ones stay to learn about the place and themselves.

Backpackers dismiss it as "too touristy" and flee to Pto. Angel, where they join a huge tribe of other gringos. They miss the point.

Travel writers churn out too much copy about "getting to Escondido before it's too late." Some old-timers (those who knew it in the 50's and 60's) claim it's already too late. The enlightened ones know better.

As usual, I'm contrary. Of course, I consider myself an old-timer, since I lived there B.S. (Before the Sewer). When I left town, the main street was dirt, but signs of progress" were already there: sewer pipes. Before long, the joyous sound of flushing would be heard throughout town.

Puerto (as its lovers call it) will never be ruined. It will change, as will we all, but it will hold onto its character. What attracts folks is the outside, the natural beauty. What keeps them is something hidden, *escondido*. Beauty fades; substance doesn't.

Most writers mention the **Santa Fe Hotel**. It's not because it's the only luxury hotel in town (not anymore). It's because it's a bastion of civility perched against a backdrop of raw, powerful nature.

The manager, Paul Nunn Cleaver, has a presence that any good hotelier anywhere in the world would be proud to have. The Santa Fe doesn't reflect his personality: it maintains the one Paul knows it should have. It has the soul of Puerto.

The **Santa Fe** (PH: (958) 2-0170) is perched on the east end of Marinero beach. It has a unique, Caribbean atmosphere with its bungalows, and several buildings spread dotting a tropical garden and pool. It's hard to believe you're in a hotel and not at some rich uncle's house.

Paul introduced us to several guests, then bravely left while one eagle-eyed journalist and beady-eyed me asked them questions about the place.

They were a mixed bag, ranging from Tim, a Florida surfer, Nancy, a 60's child who hasn't lost the child within, to Arlyne Grazer and John Refi, who mostly bopped about the world.

John & Arlyne have come back to Puerto and the Santa Fe for 3 years. "It's tranquil. This is the best hotel in the world." They have the sophistication, time and money to comparison-shop luxury hotels worldwide. I didn't dispute them.

Tim, the surfer says P.E. is "... Hawaii without the hassle."

Nancy Beckham, from Dallas, personifies what is right about Pto. Escondido.

23

She was a child of the 60's. She'd been to P.E. B.S. and fallen under its spell. Hollywood's siren lured her west. She's a singer who caught the wave of fame and fortune. She was being groomed to take over for Grace Slick. The 60's were kind to her.

Things change fast in the fast lane. Hollywood's beneficence turned to California cutthroat. It was hard to come back home to Texas, after being a minor god in the promised land, but she did.

She started a restaurant in Dallas, "Brazos" and did well. She came back to Puerto to see what part of herself she'd left there. This time instead of sleeping on the beach, or in a hammock hotel, she was staying at the first class hotel.

Instead of a backpack, she brought her daughter, Paige. Nancy hoped to share that special, inexplicable something about herself with her most special daughter who was another part of her.

Like Puerto, she'd changed over the years. Like many of us who decried the "plastic" society of our parents, she paid with plastic money.

Yet, she was not more *ruined* than Puerto. They both had superficial changes, both were more affluent, but both were just as real today as they were 20 years ago.

There's a saying in Puerto, "If you watch the sunset from Marinero beach and see the rooster's tail (the spume from a breaking wave when it fans out like a rooster's tail), it will land on your heart. You will always come back to this place."

That rooster had perched on the hearts of Paul, Arlyne, John, Nancy and me. It would plant itself in Tim and Paige before dawn the next day. They would keep coming back and keep Puerto Escondido what it was; always has been and always will be — a place where wounded hearts heal and calloused ones soften. That's not something that changes with the addition of a few hotels.

The great thing about my job is that I get to meet interesting folks. The sad thing is, I never get to *know* them.

Pto. Angel

Pto. Angel, Oax., is just down the road a piece from Pto. Escondido in miles, but light-years away in character.

It's home to one of the most pleasant hotels in Mexico. Nurtured by the slow pace of this fishing village, a loving couple turned a desert canyon into a tropical jungle.

La Posada Cañón Devata has catwalks, cats, sculptured paths, gentle bills and a meditation chapel with images of Eastern holy men.

It's a place out of place and time, and one of the most pleasant experiences of my young life. If you're short on peace & serenity, (as I was) you might find some here. Write Suzanne & Mateo López, owners, at Aptdo. Postal #74, Pochutla, Oax 70900.

They have no phone but don't need one. If you are truly advanced, you can reserve a living space by telepathy. I'm not, but they let me stay anyway.

Pto. Angel is 43 miles east on Hwy #200 of P.E.; 16 miles west of Huatulco, then a few miles south. The drive's pleasant, easy. It's a good example of the really unusual places you can visit only when you drive.

If you like the fast lane, speed on by to Huatulco. Angel appeals to a special kind of person.

A comfortable, modern hotel, facing the bay is the **Soraya**. It has nice views, a good restaurant and a very pleasant manager. It's a good deal. They don't have a phone, either.

Angel's reputation is mixed. Many are attracted because it has a nudist beach. Of course, nothing like that crossed my mind when I visited!

Travel writing is serious business and I don't have time to enjoy myself. I only went in order to accurately report the situation. The binoculars were for scouting out "topes".

"Unspoiled" and "rustic" describe Angel. Not all the streets are paved; not all the hotels have servibars. You'll see some old hippies, still lost in the ozone; some European budget travellers, and regular tourists who like the offbeat.

Mateo was a fisherman, raised there. He met Suzanne, from the U.S., got married; changed his life. That's typical, so far.

How he changed is notable. He became a real ecologist (one who did something about his beliefs, even though it meant censure from his peers). They installed a recycling system for the hotel water. It naturally filters, then feeds the acres of healthy plants via drip irrigation.

They serve an ample veggie feast at the communal dinners. Mateo is a strong man, in every way that I know about (and some far beyond me), but he speaks gently, thoughtfully.

Suzanne is alive and lights up the

place with her flashes of humor. She's a good hotelier, and bounces up and down to insure that everything runs smoothly.

We talked of many things, princes and kings, under the thatched roof dining palapa. Two long tables were filled with guests. A gentle breeze slipped over us through the *no-walls* that didn't keep us from nature.

We shared humor, philosophy and world-views. I learned what a difference a couple of committed regular folks can do to change the way we all live. They didn't know it, but they taught me a great deal about myself. We're all teachers; we're all students.

Darkness enveloped us; the other diners retired, and I was still listening to these two treasures who were raising children and taking care of a little piece of the world while being in love.

We shook hands, hugged, bid each other pleasant dreams. They went off, hand in hand, to their home. I shuffled off to my cabana.

I have a lot and don't waste time on envy but sadness caught up with me on the dark, overgrown path back to my empty room.

No matter what I had, I knew I would never have their simplicity, their simple goodness. All a man like me can do is recognize those blessed people when he meets them and be grateful for their presence.

§§§§§§§§§§§§§§§§§§§§§

Tourism informed me today that **La Pesca, Tamps.** (one of my favorite places) will be the newest "mega project". Two weeks ago, both the very nice hunting-fishing camps, **Campo La Pesca** (PH: 800-331-0479, (512) 541-1142) & Cavi del Río's place, **La Marina del Río** (PH: (512) 630-0138, 631-2220) were full of happy hunters.

More families are driving to Mexico. Today, I sent a nice lady and her lovely daughter there for a weekend. Take your family on your next driving trip.

Tripshare links Mexico fans who want to go with a kindred soul & it's free. Write Tripshare P.O. Box 310, McAllen, TX 78502.

§§§§§§§§§§§§§§§§§§§§§

"Mexico Mike" drives Mexico and writes Sanborn's Travelog — often at the same time.

Tourism

Sunday, September 23, 1990

I know y'all are wondering what effect Hurricane Diana had on the Gulf coast. So was my boss, so he re-routed me back from Oaxaca to Veracruz and up Hwy #180 to Mc-Allen. It slammed into Tuxpan on Aug. 7. The roads are okay, except for a couple of 20 mile stretches around Tuxpan, Naranjos, and north of Tampico. It's like it was a few years ago. Don't go too fast and it'll be okay.

There's a bypass around Veracruz, and two Extra gas stations. Motels springing up like mushrooms, between there and Nautla.

The **Quinta Alicia** trailer park near Nautla — one of the nicest in Mexico — is still beautiful.

There's Extra gas in Nautla. Previously, you had to go off the road eight miles to Martínez de la Torre for it. The same fellow owns both stations. Business is so good, he put it in Nautla three months ago. More people are driving! Extra is so plentiful, it's hardly worth worrying about any more.

The new "Magna Sin" has been introduced and will eventually replace "Extra." It's more refined (not better-mannered) with higher octane. If you've been putting off a driving trip because of a shortage of unleaded gas, your excuse is gone.

This is true everywhere. I logged Hwy #180 only six months before and it's changed for the better. Things are changing fast in Mexico.

Keeping the *Travelog* — Sanborn's mile-by-smile highway guide — accurate is darned tough.

The abundance of unleaded gasoline is a good example of the commitment the **Lic. Pedro Joaquín Caldwell** has to surface tourism. The government knows that surface tourism has increased greatly in the last few years, while air tourists have only marginally increased.

My good friend, **Lic. Gilberto Calderón Romo**, the director of surface tourism in Mexico City, and the former director of the Green Angels and chief of caravans, **Marcelino** — who is so friendly and popular that he's known by his first name, originated a great idea to increase driving tourists. How's this for a motto: "To go to Mexico — fly. To know Mexico — drive!"?

The undersecretary of Tourism, **Carlos Camacho Gaos**, put it best, "Sun and sand are no longer enough — travelers worldwide seek more than a one-dimensional vacation experience."

Thanks to the efforts of the people above and **Jorge Gamboa** and my fishing partner **Rolando García**, of the Mexican Office of Tourism in Houston, they'll take the rest of Mexico on the road. In early 1991, hoteliers, tourism delegates and others will tour Texas to show everybody that Mexico has a lot to offer besides beaches.

"Mordida" is being replaced with

pride in Mexican character. It would be Pollyanna-ish to say that a great change like this can occur overnight, but much has changed since the Salinas' administration. I've been around Mexico for over 20 years and I'm impressed. My dealings with police and government officials make me feel that a fresh breeze is blowing out the old ways. Mexicana pride shows in their actions. **Mexico has much to be proud of, most of all its people.**

We all hope the developers of these new areas on the Gulf realize that **unique developments that preserve the character of the area are more appealing than another Cancún.**

Next week, Tuxpan. Then we visit Tecolutla, where Bridgette Bardot and I slept (not together, silly).

"Mexico Mike" updates Sanborn's Travelog when not fantasizing about French women. Now he's looking for Puerto Vallarta.

28

Tuxpan

Sunday, September 30, 1990

Aug. 7, 1990 — Hurricane Diana fooled a lot of people and hit Tuxpan, Ver. I talked to the new manager, **Jorge Pérez Basanez**, of the not so old **Hotel Tajín** (Carret A. Cabos KM 2.5, Aptdo Postal 224, Tuxpam, Ver. PH: (783) 4-2260, 5-2312) about it. It's 1.5 miles southeast of the bridge over the Rio Tuxpam. No, I didn't misspell it. The Totonacs spelled it that way. It means "place of the rabbit".

He had a bird's eye view, so to speak. My favorite thing about this elegant hotel was the panoramic view from the giant glass windows in the restaurant. They ran from door to ceiling, perhaps 40 feet. Hotels with glass walls should not face the Gulf.

The eye passed right over the Tajín. Jorge was on the phone with his boss, who told him the "tropical storm" was nearby. As the 40 foot glass walls came tumbling down around him he politely informed the boss that the "storm" had been upgraded. His boss wanted Jorge to keep him informed — every hour. Bosses can be so demanding.

Sr. Pérez is a philosophical man, fitting for the lawyer he is. He prefers working with tourists. He said, "It was a good thing. The hotel needed a face-lift, so it just made it easier to start over." The Tajín is a grand hotel, built on a commanding crook in the river, like a sentinel. It had been owned by a union pension fund, but was recently sold to a private company. The new owners are remodeling stem to stern and will open in Dec., 1990 or Jan., 1991.

Jorge, an erudite and thoughtful man, showed us the grounds. They cover several acres with lush tropical gardens and manicured grass lawns. There's an Olympic-sized pool, several cabañas in addition to the five-story hotel. Cantinflas has a house on them.

I asked about a jacuzzi. For those of you who don't know me, I was a prisoner of California once. The only thing I kept from California when I left was a love of jacuzzis. It's my duty to find every one in Mexico and rate it. Mexicans often have private jacuzzis (or spas) in suites, but public ones are rare.

Jorge told me about the presidential jacuzzi. I said regular folks like me and you were more likely to stay there if he had a public one. By the time we left, he promised it would be installed. He invited me back for the grand opening, when the President of Mexico will be there. I'm sure I won't get to jacuzzi with Mr. Salinas, but I'm counting on using the new public one. Drivers in particular appreciate a hot whirlpool after a hard day. Many of Sanborn's customers decide where to stay based on whether I've told them a hotel has a jacuzzi or tubs.

The name will change. "Tajín" means windy place — no longer a funny joke. I'll let you know as soon as I know the new name.

Tuxpan(m) is a laid-back riverside/seaside town with friendly folks, a nice plaza and plenty of hotels. Another is the **Sara**, (Guarizurieta #44, PH: 4.0010, 4.0059). It's new and has a pool on the roof. Rooms are spacious. Downtown, across from the plaza are the **Plaza, Reforma, Florida**. They all have character. They're spitting distance from each other. On the bypass is the nice **Plaza Palmas**, with tennis courts and ample parking.

"Mexico Mike" is out "working" again. He claimed Puerto Vallarta needed updating for Sanborn's "Travelog". We know he's lying on the beach and lying to his boss, and we wish we could get away with it.

Tecolutla

Sunday, October 7, 1990

Tecolutla, Ver. is a great get-away place. Brigitte Bardot and I got away there. We both slept at the **Hotel-Balneario Tecolutla** (PH: (784) 5-0901 or 5-0763).

For those of you with dirty minds, I didn't say we shared a bed. In fact, a few years passed between our visits.

If you're driving south, on Hwy #180, turn east 34.5 miles south of **Poza Rica**. If you're heading north, turn at 24 miles north of El Faro Junction.

It'll take about half an hour to drive through the little town of **Gutiérrez Zamora**, which is white-wash-clean and tidy, and on to the beach via an OK blacktop.

The road passes through some rich farm and ranch country before dead-ending into the best hotel in town.

B.B., as those of us who grew up with Ms. Bardot are wont to call her, was there to film a movie, *Viva María*. I was there for the same reason you will be — it's a great place to enjoy the beach with half the crowds and a more restful atmosphere than the Island.

If you remember **Padre Island** before it was *condo-ized*, you'll lust after Tecolutla! Remember long stretches of white sand, dunes taller than your ten year-old head and gently-heavy breakers? That was there then and that's Tecolutla now.

Of course, there's not as much action in this sleepy little town. I couldn't find a disco, or a loud bar. I missed the tacky T-shirt shops, too. No drunken kids tried to run me down, or yell obscenities at me. I really missed all those delights of civilization! If a wild time's your thing, bring your own, or better yet, stay home.

The action time is during the **Feast of San Bartolo**, from Aug. 18-26. We were fortunate to hit it and it's a neat deal. You won't see a lot of pomp put on to impress the tourists, but you will see a genuine Mexican festival.

The square is ringed by folks selling chances on everything from packages of gum to $50 bills.

There are rides that couldn't possibly be as exciting as the paintings decorating them. Kids run about everywhere, a sure sign that this is the real thing.

Walk two blocks off the square, towards the ever-pounding Gulf, and you'll be offered more ways to fill your gullet than you could try in a week. We elected for a Mom-&-Pop place on Calle Matamoros. All of 'em have good fish, shrimp and oysters.

The **Hotel-Balneario Tecoluta** (Calle Matamoros S/N) doesn't have, or need, a street number. It sits at the end of the road, a silent, imposing sentinel, guarding the beach from uninvited invasion. It's a three-story place with 72 rooms and a newer and older section. Guess which one has A/C?

It used to be quite a place when balnearios (spas or mineral springs) were in fashion. Today, it maintains an air of faded elegance that draws those of us who are trapped in the wrong time to it. The pools are big and sparkling. I'm not sure they cured anything in me, but I've been feeling pretty good lately. The dining room is immense, capable of holding the full capacity of the hotel and a few friends. Prices are reasonable and the service excellent.

I'd written in the *Travelog* that the manager spoke English, French and Spanish. That was last year. Today the manager is **Wilfredo Vassallo**, and he speaks English and Spanish.

You can bed there for $25-$35, if there are two of you. If there's only one of you, I'm sorry. You should have signed up for **Tripshare**.

Tecoluta is just one more of the delightful get away places that you can only get to by driving. You could be there in one very hard day, or two comfortable ones. If you're coming home from Veracruz or Mexico City, it makes a nice break. Maybe I'll see you there!

HIGHWAY UPDATES

Phil Templin gave us the following: **MAGNA SIN**, the replacement for Extra, is available just about everywhere on the Gulf coast. Tuxpan has it in town, not on highway. Palma Sola has it. Veracruz has it. Tampico was sold out but he filled up in San Fernando.

I saw it all over the West Coast.

The *other Nelson* saw it between D.F. - Pátzcuaro.

If you haven't been driving Mexico for fear of not finding unleaded gas, get goin' or get a new excuse!

Hwy #180 *rumply-bumpy* between Tuxpan & Tampico. Not bad, but slow down. Some potholes between Lerdo and Alvarado. Road crews are fixing all this. Hwy #131, bad shape from hurricane. Avoid.

Hwy #54 between Guadajara and Zacatecas — there's a bad detour. Go by way of Aguascalientes-Lagos. Check with Sanborn's or Green Angels in Mexico.

"Mexico" Mike is back home, writing Sanborn's Travelog. We bet he'll break from the pressure, and leave for Mexico soon.

The Day of the Dead

Sunday, October 4, 1990

One of the most interesting Mexican festivals turns death into an event of light, sound, and fantasy — and it's coming soon!

Oaxaca and the island of *Janitzio* (in the middle of Lago Pátzcuaro), are the best-known Mexican places for celebrating **The Day of the Dead**.

Like many things in Mexico, it's something more than it appears. The "day" is really two days: **Nov. 1 and 2.**

I recently rolled in from the "Deep South" of Mexico with Eric the Heroic and Mike the Zamba. There honestly couldn't be a better time to drive to Oaxaca.

Unleaded gas is nearly everywhere and the roads are in fine shape. Take a week off and frolic with the spirits in Oaxaca.

This festival was celebrated by the Indians of central Mexico before Cortez ever set foot on our continent. The Tarascan, Nahua and Otomi Indians have strong traditions about this religious festival.

They believe that the deceased come back to visit their relatives on these two days. Sometimes they offer advice, sometimes they just come by to chat. No matter, families prepare a feast for the hungry souls sure to drop in.

They sanctify their homes and graveyards with flickering candles and smoking incense. These help the departed find their way to and fro.

Brightly decorated skulls (mostly plastic, but not all) show up everywhere! Skull-shaped candies delight the kiddies.

We may think this macabre, until we understand that other peoples' ways of looking at things are not wrong — just different. The Nahuas didn't think the skull was a symbol of death: for them it was symbol of the promise of a new life. It was a common form of ornamentation. Think of it as a pre-Columbian happy face.

Mexicans, too, regard death differently. For many, it's the ultimate liberation. They are proudly defiant of death, treating it with irony. Most stories about Mexico (by Gringos or Mexicans) have Death lurking in them somewhere.

One of my earliest heroes (after Dan Sanborn and B. Traven) was Malcom Lowry, whose *Under the Volcano* gives a chilling, haunting picture of a man and country obsessed by death. I hope your journey doesn't end like his!

The day before is the festival of the little dead, the children who've died. Devoted parents set up altars in their homes and cover them with candies and toys. Even dead kids want to have a good time.

The next day, folks spread candles and food feasts at cemeteries all around. At dusk, church bells will toll ceaselessly, relentlessly, through the night. Their haunting peals will "wake the dead", calling them from their graves.

As with any festival in Mexico, there'll be fireworks. Boy will there be fireworks! Powerful explosions of sound and color will mark the way for any soul who's lost.

The fireworks will culminate with the traditional Mexican "tower of pyro-power." Weeks before artisans construct a multi-tiered wooden frame. Then they meticulously intertwine thousands of firecrackers on each level. The higher the level, the more powerful and magnificent the explosion. They range from a few feet to many hundreds of feet tall.

From one lit wick, this layered pyre will detonate itself, tier by tier. At the height of its death rattle, it spits out a wheel of kaleidoscopic explosions that shrieks, cries, cackles, crackles, whistles and banshee-screams into the night.

Sometimes, an eerie silence will prevail. The black night will be broken by few human sounds. Only the incessant tolling of the bells — like an iron heartbeat — seems alive.

The area code is (951). One of the most beautiful hotels in Mexico is the **Presidente-Oaxaca** (PH: 6-0611). Even if you don't stay there (& it's often full), visit the restaurant and grounds.

The old **Victoria** (PH: 5-2633) is one of my favorites. They've remodeled and have the best view of the city. The **Misión-Oaxaca** (PH: 5-0100) is a good value, as are all the Misions.

The **Señorial** (PH: 6-3933) is on the zócalo and a good deal.

The **Misión de los Angeles** (PH: 5-1500) is luxurious.

El Asador Vasco has elegant dining on the zócalo. For cheaper eats, try the **Restaurant Quickly**, a few blocks off the square.

Many thanks to **Ing. Juan Arturo López Ramos**, Director of Tourism in Oaxaca, for his erudite help in my research.

Have a great time raising the dead, and remember that *Tripshare* (our free ride-sharing service) can keep you from having to go alone!

"Mexico" Mike writes Sanborn's Travelog, a guide of all the highways of Mexico, when he's not playing with Death. Some say he is dead, but that's just his grave personality.

34

Padre Harold Miracle

Sunday, October 21, 1990

Padre Harold bounced in the other day. He'd been rolling up and down Hwy #85, in his ancient motorhome. He's the only person I know who's exorcised a Mercedes-Benz garage.

I could tell from the impish smile that belied his choirboy face that he had a good story for me.

You think "round" when you see him. He has a cherub's face behind John Denver steel-rimmed glasses. His smile makes you want to trust him. I reckon that's why he's good at what he does.

He's one of a small army of missionaries who flock to Mexico. Some are affiliated with major churches and many, like Padre Harold, aren't. He was once, but that's a long story.

Often, one of 'em, or group of 'em will "adopt" a town or village, help build a school or church, while trying to add new souls to their flock.

The good padre has a congregation in San Luis Potosí state near a village called San Juan Sin Agua. God must have a Mexican sense of humor, because it was the only village in the neighborhood that had water during the current drought.

He mixes preaching with practicality. He teaches folks how to read and write and explains fundamental principles of health and hygiene to "his" towns.

He made a miracle happen recently. He'll deny it, of course, but to me, and to his flock, he's a rainmaker.

Recently, large black rain clouds loomed in the distance. Harold said the rains would come. The farmers knowingly shook their heads and said they would not.

"You must pray," the padre said.

"We have prayed for a year and there has been no rain."

"Then there must be something wrong with the way you are praying," asserted the padre.

"But, padre, there is only one way to pray." The farmers were beginning to think that the good padre was touched.

He smiled his cherubic smile. "Who do you pray to?"

The old farmers looked at each other and said together, "to *Diosito*, of course."

Harold just smiled the more. "That is the problem!" he exclaimed.

The farmers were puzzled and so may you be, so I'll explain. *Dios* means God, but adding *ito* makes it a diminutive, like "little one." Thus *Diosito* means "little God." Normally, it is a sign of affection.

So, you can see why the campesinos used it. They were on a friendly, affectionate footing with their Maker.

"What you have done," the padre explained "is to ask a powerful favor from God, then insult him by

35

calling him a little God. No wonder you get no favors!"

The farmers thought for a few moments, and saw the logic. "But what are we to do?"

"Ask His Son to intercede for you. Pray to *Jesusito* for help."

The whole village prayed during Padre Harold's service that night. In the middle of the night it rained. Man did it rain!

It rained like hell, until late the next morning. Harold unrolled the plastic awning of his motorhome to catch the rainwater. He helped the villagers gather buckets and tarps to catch as much as they could.

For a village that had to pay to have all their water trucked in this was truly a Godsend.

"You're a miracle-maker," I exclaimed.

Harold stopped smiling. "I don't know how much good I've done. I just do what I can. I work with those who have nothing and help to make their own lives better. I don't know how much longer I can do it."

I'd never seen him down before. We're all affected by worldly concerns.

He usually made four trips a year to "his" villages. This year he could afford one.

His only source of funds has always been donations. Sanborn's began helping him a long time ago and still does. Sadly, many folks who've helped over the years have retired and have less to help with or have gone to their greater reward.

Heck even *pinche* (cheap) Mike was touched by his story. I'm willing to pitch in a few dead presidents to help him out. I'll give his address to anybody who wants to help.

About the Mercedes-Benz garage. It's near Corpus and was the only one with some tool he needed for his old motorhome. When he stopped in to borrow one, the mechanics said to him the place was possessed.

During his time as a minister of an organized church, Padre Harold had learned the exorcism rite. He performed it, and the weird happenings in the garage ceased. Those mechanics hold him in reverence, and now work on his buggy for free.

"Mexico" Mike edits Sanborn's Travelog, a highway guide to Mexico, when he's not being generous. He swears his computer, Traven, is possessed.

36

My First in Mazatlán

Sunday, July 15, 1990

After 40, firsts of anything are exquisite, if rare, experiences. My last "first" was in Mazatlán, Mexico.

A desert rat born in Las Cruces, NM, I grew up with a reverence for water. Elephant Butte Reservoir began a rite of passage that ended on the Pacific Ocean.

Old-timers know this Pacific port as the "Billfish Capital of the World." First-time fishermen may like it because the fishing's so good that even "Mexico Mike" can catch 'em here.

Whether you go to fish or play in the sun, Mazatlán can please you. Sun, sand, and stark mountains that rise from the water to provide dramatic backdrops for tropical sunsets are abundant. You can get away from it all or be with the para-sailing crowd — you've got a choice. Maybe your search for something unnameable will end there. Mine did.

From boyhood, I was in love with fishing and always dreamed of the day when I'd go to the blue water and manhandle a marlin. Don't we all?

Deep-sea fishing's a bargain. For under $100, you can sample a rich man's sport. Numerous record fish have been caught there.

Driving's easy and safe. Don't believe what you've heard from folks who've never done it. Government employees called Green Angels patrol the roads just looking for stranded tourists to help. Leave any U.S. crossing & you'll be there in only 3 days. From El Paso, or New Mexico, it'll take you through some of the most spectacularly serene country in Mexico. Take your time and enjoy.

Get Mexican insurance before you go. **NO U.S.** insurance is valid in Mexico. The Mexican government is promoting driving now and unleaded gas is available, though it helps to know where to look. A Sanborn's *"Travelog"* (highway guide) is invaluable. On the way you can frolic in the mountains and explore old silver-mining towns.

For most of us, life interrupts our fishing. We keep putting it off — it's too expensive, ... maybe next year. One day we wake up and all we have is crabgrass, dusty fishing rods and a spouse who thinks salmon eggs are appetizers.

At 22, either an alien spaceship beamed me, or I just lost the knack of catching fish. I was fishing-sterile. I didn't catch fish in most every state in the Union, several Caribbean nations, the **AMAZON**, for God's sake, and Canada.

Even Mexico shunned me. If you know Mexican fishing, you'll realize how pitiful I was when I say that I **DIDN'T** catch bass in Lake Guerrero, Tamaulipas when it opened. Sportsmen called it the hottest bass lake in the world. I couldn't catch a cold.

At 39 & 11/12ths, I was aboard one of Bill Hemphil's deep-sea fishing boats, 10 miles offshore of Mazatlán, staring at the bluest water I'd ever seen. A taciturn Mexican captain named Juan held my fate in his hands. I wasn't worried, he'd been working these waters with the Starfleet when I still got lucky.

These 44 foot boats were ideal for these waters. They all met U.S. Coast Guard safety requirements, though we were a thousand miles from the nearest U.S. Coast Guard station.

Here's a primer of deep sea fishing. The mate (Jorge) baits the hook with live 5 inch mullet. He drops the line behind the trolling boat. We were running 2 outriggers (long rods with artificial lures to attract the fish and wake us up). Usually, he hits the artificials, then the real stuff.

If you're afraid (as I was) of some giant of the deep pulling the expensive rod out of your hands, don't be. The mate won't even let you touch the rod until he's hooked the fish, you've sat in the "fighting chair" and he's secured the butt of the rod in a steel swivel at its base. Till then, you can snooze. I did.

At 11:47, our sunny lull was shattered. Something hit one of the outriggers. The captain slowed. The mate slid down the ladder to the deck. The starboard rod bent, then "zinged". Jorge grabbed it, and expertly set the hook. Somebody threw me into the fighting chair. Jorge walked the rod over, secured it in the chair clamp. Everyone stared at me.

Are you one of those folks who forget little things? Me, too. I forgot to ask how I was supposed to "catch" a fish. All I knew was that there was something on the end of a quarter of a mile of line that was an important part of my life.

Dumbly, I reacted by instinct and pulled up. The line went taut and then went singing away. I was lucky. It didn't break. The rod was pulled inexorably down. The camera around my neck kept banking into the rod. I felt excited, stupid and frantic.

Then she sailed several feet into the air, her blue-silver body sleek and her iridescent sail surreal. Time stopped — I was serene. I didn't relate that majestic creature to the force at the end of my line. She slipped noiselessly into the water and my line sang out. It was so captivating that it had to be a "she".

Jorge grabbed my shoulder and motioned in what seemed an obscene gesture, pumping up and down. Dimly, I caught on. I was supposed to let my fish (now it was MY fish) take as much line as needed when she wanted to run and lower the tip and reel like crazy when she was resting or flying.

And she did fly! Once she stood on her tail and waltzed across the water as if in a lusty dance for my attention. When she appeared, I forgot I was fishing. We communed, melded. When she dove, my body pumped and reeled, but my mind dove with her.

I felt the water rush through my gills, off my sides. I thought dimly, in images, with pain and pride blending. I felt no remorse for a life unlived, nor rancor towards the man above who was slowly wearing me out. I didn't know if I'd win or he, but somehow we ceased being competitors and became equals — each imprisoned by our environment. All things were happening in their own time and I was only a part of the larger fabric.

They tell me it was a short fight — about 20 minutes. It doesn't matter. My sailfish came aboard, exhausted, but still with spirit. Her stomach, red and stringy, trailed from her lance-like bill. Even if we'd released her, she might not have lived. She was tall, seven feet, and slim, 90 pounds.

"Catch and release" hasn't caught on in Mazatlán, as it has in the Baja. That means letting 'em go. The thrill's in the catching, not in the pictures later.

For those concerned about decimating the sailfish, marlin etc. population, take solace in the fact that Japanese "long-liners" (fishing boats that trail 20-40 **MILES** of baited lines) take more sailfish in one day (about 7,000) than sport fishermen take in a year. The Mexican government's starting to do something about it, but it's a fact of life (or death).

You have the rights to the fish, but if you give it to the captain, he'll sell most of it and donate the rest to a jail or orphanage. The captain depends on tips ($20-$50) and the fish to support his family. If you get stiffed by Mother Nature, don't do the same to the captain, please. Stuffing 'em is expensive.

It'll cost you $69 plus tip to share the boat. If you want the whole thing to yourself, (as a serious angler will), plan on $300. This is still cheaper than across the Gulf in Baja.

There ain't no guarantees in fishin', friend. You may not catch anything, but the odds are in your favor. Bill's boats average two fish per boat per day. You can fish all year, but May is the beginning of the good times. Sailfish, and marlin are best from June to October. Reservations are "reel" smart. Call Gerónimo (Jerry) Jerkins at 1-800-633-3085 in San Antonio Texas as soon as you know you're going. He's a straight shooter.

Billfish bite year-round. May to November is the peak season for black and blue marlin & sailfish. Winter is for striped marlin & sailfish. The rainy season is from August to September. Naturally, those are the best fishing months. Don't worry, the rain's warm and soft.

I've bedded in Mazatlán from the Golden Zone to the old section, called "Olas Altas" and each has its advantages.

If you're going first-class, the elegant **El Cid Resort and Golf Club**, runs about $90 and is worth it. It has swimming pools, a waterfall, tennis and quiet rooms with tubs. I don't sing praises of swank hotels unless they earn them. You don't always get what you pay for, but this time you do. Packages are available that will lighten the tariff. PH: Mexico

— (011-52) (678) 3-3333. In the
U.S. — 1-800-446-1069, or 1-800-
525-1925.

I've bunked at the old **Belmar** in
Olas Altas section for about $20. I
honeymooned there, but that was
pushing it. It has a faded grandeur
and the rooms remind you of a
ships'. Some have balconies and
you can hear a gentle lapping of
waves after the traffic quiets about
9 PM. PH: Mexico — (011-52)
(678) 2-0799.

The **De Cima** is an old-time fa-
vorite in-between the two in loca-
tion, price and features. It faces the
beach, has a pool and is a solid
place, run by the De Cima family.
PH: Mexico — (011-52) (678) 2-
7300.

No matter why you came,
Mazatlán will give you something
to take home. It always has for me.

Driving to the Copper Canyon

Sunday, October 28, 1990

If you've ever heard the siren call of a new road beckoning you, or like Joseph Conrad longed for the "...blank spots on the map", then I've got a road for you!

Barranca de Cobre, (the Copper Canyon), has scenery you can't see anywhere else in North America. Accessible only by train tour since the '60's, you can now drive there! Like the airplane opening Hawaii in the '50's, this will change its character, so see it now.

Leave your preconceptions in your other suitcase! Eat at a seafood restaurant in the prairie..a 4 star restaurant next to a bus station. Instead of adobe, folks live in log houses and retired railcars. Listen to Mennonites speaking Spanish; the impassioned wail of a train whistle echoing through mountains never scaled by man.

West of Chihuahua, Chih. the canyon stretches 1,500 km through the almost impassable Sierra Madre Occidental Mountains to Los Mochis, Sinaloa and the Bay of California.

It holds millions of acres so rugged, so inhospitable, that no roads trespass and many of the people live an almost stone-age existence. Known as "those who run fast", they run marathon distances over mountainous terrain for sport and necessity. They are among the few people on earth who **run down** deer!

Sheer stone walls drop vertically for 6,000 feet. In winter, you'll wear snowsuits on the top and halter tops at the bottom, only hours away. It's a land of contradictions and anomalies.

Until Nov. 24th, 1961, this untamed region was accessible only on foot and muleback. After nearly 100 years, the visionary American engineer, John Kinsey Owens' dream became reality. (More about him later.) 25 years later, a highway, the "Gran Vision", opened to Creel, Chih.

Years before, I rode the famous train through the canyon. Then, I was too bound by schedules to get off and see it closer. Now I drive Mexico so I can go where I want, when I want.

You can get there from the border crossing in McAllen. Take Hwy #40 through Monterrey, Saltillo, Torreón, turn north on Hwy #45 into Chihuahua. Allow two days.

Driving in Mexico is and isn't like driving Stateside. It's a more laissez-faire approach to driving. "Go with the flow." I've done it for 20 years and love it. If you drive in L.A. or Dallas, then you know that there are times when traffic flows to rhythm. Buck it: you're anxious and in trouble. Catch it: go with it, and the other cars are partners in an intricate ballet. That's driving in Mexico.

Here's how to get out of **Chihuahua City:** head south, aiming for the top of the hill. Pass the prison and Pancho Villa's house. Turn west at the dead end. Sanborn's has a detailed guide. Once out, go west towards **Cuauhtémoc.**

Didn't expect to find a seafood restaurant in the middle of the high desert plateau, did you? In a log cabin, yet! On Sunday, it's packed with Chihuahenses families.

Stoop for the low roof and step down as you enter. Warmth envelopes you in the moist darkness. Smells of meat and seafood pull you closer to the stove in the middle of the room. You'll think you've stepped back in time and are in a sod-house on the 1800's Kansas prairie. The shrimp's great — better (and cheaper!) than in Cancún or Mazatlán. It must improve with the aging on the trip from the ocean. A word of caution — don't try the "sopa oso" (bear soup). It's so hot you can hardly bear to eat it.

If you stop here, you'll be politely ignored — a mountain custom. That's different than the "typical" warmth of Southern Mexicans. These folks are just as friendly, but you have to make the first move.

The only large town on the route, Cuauhtemoc, is noted for Mennonite cheese. These folks migrated to Chihuahua during the early part of the century and settled all along Hwy #16. Sewing dresses and big bonnets for the women, black wide brimmed hats and coats for the men. Yep, these are the real folks, living their own way in Mexico just like they do anywhere else.

The **Equus** is a 4 star restaurant, with white-coated waiters, across from the bus station. Don't park at the curb beside the bus station — I did and had to wait for a bus to board and unboard because I had his spot. Nobody got upset; the nice folks just looked at me sadly.

After Cuauhtemoc, the road changes from rolling hills to twisty mountain drives. Log cabins, logging camps and railroad cars where people live are only landmarks. Watch ahead!

"Mexico" Mike finally found Pto. Vallarta and all of its beautiful women. He says that he will be back next week, as usual — wreaking havoc and updating Sanborn's Travelogs. Stay tuned.

42

AAA

I hate to interrupt our peaceful journey to the Copper Canyon, but AAA warned me it's not safe to drive in Mexico!

Gee, when a big organization like the American Automobile Association (AAA) warns an average guy like me, I listen.

A friend sent me an AAA advisory his AAA agent gave him. It kept eight other couples from going to Mexico at all.

The memo states that AAA has "embarked on an in-depth re-evaluation of AAA's Mexico travel package."

Why? "In light of two unsettling incidents experienced by a member of our field staff."

Gosh, what happened? It must have been pretty serious for a worldwide organization to actively bash an entire country!

If you have a bad experience and tell your friends, that's your right. They know what your opinion is worth.

An organization, a newspaperman, or anyone with the ability to shape public opinion, though, is different.

Others depend on us for intelligent analysis. We have a responsibility to get our facts straight; use informed sources; and deliver unbiased recommendations — or make our bias known.

You know my bias — I love Mex-

ico. I'm also a realist who knows it not perfect. I've spent years getting to know the country.

Today, I drive 20,000 miles a year checking road conditions, rating hotels, restaurants, and general tourist interests.

I'm careful because I know that about 250,000 people will read what I write. That's how many people drive Mexico each year with Sanborn's Travelog.

AAA influences many more people who know nothing about Mexico. Their first (and often last) source of information is AAA. They have worldwide influence. Millions accept their opinion as fact.

For years they've discouraged driving in Mexico, by denying unleaded gas was available, when that was not true.

Now this! This venomous memo advises their agents, "Please be sure that your membership preparing to drive ... is fully aware of the precautions .. in the 'A Few Words of Caution' section of the Mexico Travel Guide."

They claim driving's unsafe on Hwys #15 & #1 in Sinaloa, Hwy #40 from Durango to Mazatlán, and Hwy #57 *(get this)* from Matehuala to San Luis Potosí! Gosh, that makes it pretty hard to get anywhere!

Here's their justification for condemning an entire country. In one "unsettling incident", a Pemex sta-

43

tion had an "inoperative gas pump gauge". (Does that surprise any of us who've driven Mexico? Of course not! It happens from time to time.)

Worse yet, "extortion" occurred at this Pemex! **Come on, guys!** Some gas jockey will try to get you once in a while — even in the U.S. **Who hasn't ever been short-changed at least once in the U.S.**

Lordy, there was "a very intimidating crowd" at the station. **Good grief!** It was probably a bunch of kids who wanted to wash the windshield, or heaven forbid, check the air and oil.

Folks, while gassing up at a Pemex is still sometimes an adventure, it hasn't caused anyone I know a trauma.

Yes, some stations routinely "miscalculate" or have hordes of kids who are rowdy. You would be, too, if you had to scrounge for pesos the way they do. Honestly, they are the exception; not the rule.

The other "incident" involved an illegal toll collected by individuals, "posing as an immigration checkpoint (that's how they put it), dressed in uniforms ..."

To launch such a misguided attack on an entire country in the light of two dubious and relatively minor events is unpardonable.

To do so at the very time when President Salinas has made such **real strides** in curbing all forms of corruption, is incredibly poor manners.

Whenever he's heard of real incidents of corruption, he's taken ac-

tion. Mexicans are proud of him. So am I. Today Mexicans say "*todo es posible.*"

Folks, I'm sure that if the AAA heads knew about this, they'd lighten up. I corresponded with their CEO and regional chiefs in 1989. They assured me they'd cease bashing Mexico.

I guess I'm just not important enough a guy to influence them. Perhaps if you AAA members write them and let them know how you feel, they'd listen.

I'm not bashing AAA. I just wish they'd stop hurting Mexico's tourism — and economy.

Interestingly, Mexican officials wanted AAA's input on increasing surface tourism. Right now, I think they'd tell AAA where to put their input.

§§§§§§§§§§§§§§§§§§§§§§

"Mexico" Mike spends most of his young life behind the wheel in Mexico. The rest of the time he writes for several publications, including the "Mexico City News". What's left, he spends behind the eightball.

Pto. Vallarta

Sunday, November 11, 1990

When the weather here turns cold and drizzly, it's just starting to get nice in Pto. Vallarta. Let's go!

"Vallarta" as those of us in the know call it, was pretty much unknown until the 1950's. The filming of *Night of the Iguana* was the first step on its ladder of touristic success. When Liz Taylor and Richard Burton carried on like a pair of minks, it got a reputation as a hedonistic playground.

They bought playpens across the street from each other and stretched a catwalk across the street so Liz couldn't be accused of being a streetwalker. John Huston, a man who was not known for his amorous restraint, did much to promote the place with the Hollywood and Jet Set crowd.

It avoids being "touristy" like Cancún, mainly because the folks who live there are from the area and really care about their town. There are plenty of hotels, ranging from the cheap to the chic.

Getting there from McAllen or any other Texas border crossing is easy, but it will take three days. Take your time and enjoy them. Head towards Guadalajara.

You can roll through Monterrey-Saltillo, then take Hwy #54 or #57 south through Zacatecas or San Luis Potosí (then Hwy #80 to Lagos de Moreno) or amble down Hwy #35 from China and meander through the Sierra Madres towards the San Roberto Junction, then aim yourself towards Matehuala.

The Guadalajara-Tepic road is one of my least favorites, but I just heard of a neat place 52 KM north of Tepic and then 20 KM east, called **La Laguna de Santa María del Oro**. It has a crater lake 2 KM in diameter at 730 KM altitude. It's places like that which making driving the best way to really see and enjoy Mexico. The **Koala** bungalows and trailer park there look like they're peaceful and comfortable. I'm going there in December, so I'll let you know how they stack up to the mattress test.

A new road's being built which will make this a more pleasant drive, perhaps next year.

Once I got to Vallarta, I was fortunate enough to stay in one of the nicest hotels in Mexico. The **Villas Quinta Real** (PH: (322) 1-0800, FAX 1-0801, US 1-800-445-4565) are unique. Unless you're used to going first class, you may be in for a shock.

There's no "lobby". You enter an elegant, marble-floored room, take a right at the statue-fountain, and chat with a polite young man who will register you.

Martha González de Campa, the public relations manager there, showed me to my suite. Hey, it's a tough job, this travel writing, so I deserve a nice room.

Ok, I'm not the kind of guy who's used to living like the rich and famous, so I was pretty impressed. Folks, I've rested my curly-haired head on a lot of pillows, but this was the best yet.

The furniture was hand-carved in Michoacán and hand-painted in subdued pastels, with nature scenes. The bed was set into a seashell carved into the wall.

I know I'm not the smartest guy in the world, but that was the first time I couldn't find the TV in a hotel. I had to ask the maid. She giggled, then opened what I thought was a wardrobe and there it was. That's class.

If you've been reading this column, you know that I'm a jacuzzi freak. You can imagine the size of my smile when I saw the fullsized jacuzzi in my bathroom! You can also imagine my disappointment when I had it full of steaming water and couldn't find the switch to turn it on! Once again the smiling maid helped me out. That time, though, she left shaking her head.

The **Quinta Real** chain is small, with three hotels in Mexico. They're in **Guadalajara, Zacatecas & Vallarta**. They're the only Mexican chain that's a member of the **Small Luxury Hotel Association**. Everything was first class and subdued. The piped-in music was classical and the soothing sound of running water filled the halls and rooms. The staff was cordial, which you'd expect. Since I'm a sneaky guy, I walked into the kitchen area and talked to the folks who worked there as well as the maids and bellmen.

The real test of any business is how happy its employees are. If the help is surly, it doesn't matter how many jacuzzis you've got in your room. These folks seemed pleased to be there. I never had a better (*working*) time in my life, than I did there. If you're going to any of the cities with one of their hotels, give the Quinta Real chain a shot. Tell 'em Mikey likes 'em.

Next week I'll tell you about other jacuzzis and some bargains.

Many Valleyites are going to San Miguel for Thanksgiving, including me. If I train down, I'll tell you what it's like.

Welcome back, Winter Texans! Mexico has been preparing for your visits. There's plenty of unleaded gas — in fact, Mexico buys 58% of all gas exported by the U.S.

§§§§§§§§§§§§§§§§§§§§§§

"Mexico" Mike spends very little time working, but can sometimes be found at Sanborn's Mexico Insurance where he pretends to edit their highway guide — The Travelog.

46

Try Tampico

Tuesday, November 13, 1990

Try Tampico! A wonderful surprise awaits, only 6 hours south of McAllen or Brownsville, Texas. It's as lively as Veracruz — as seedy as New Orleans — it's hidden jewel is a virgin. Beach, that is. Even getting there is full of pleasant surprises!

Few North American tourists spend more than a night here. They scurry/hurry southward in search of the very things Tampico offers. I, too, was one of them — until recently.

Are you like me? Do you long to "discover" the "real" Mexico. You know — the one where the secrets of the Aztecs and Mayans and the meaning of Life are hidden? Like most searchers, I overlooked the nearby. I was impelled southward to Oaxaca, Chiapas, the Yucatan. Tamaulipas, an easy day's drive from my McAllen home couldn't hold anything of interest to a "real" Mexico rat.

Here's the straight story on driving there. The highway, (#180) needs a press agent as much as it needs repairs. Maybe more. It slithers down the Gulf coast like a flighty blacksnake. Some folks have called it names over the years, none of them polite.

There are some rough spots, and sometimes the pavement looked like it had melted then flowed back over the roadbed like lava, and they come and go. You'll just have to slow down or visit your chiropractor when you get back. The choice is yours. Mostly, it's good, solid two lane blacktop, a bit of four-lane, with enough unleaded gas to satisfy my eight cylinder guzzler. The journey ends with a majestic bridge honored by the King of Spain for an artistic achievement.

By the way, in September, 1990, Mexico began replacing "Extra" with "Magna Sin." Both my journeys and those of the hundreds of Sanborn's Insurance customers since concur: you won't have a problem finding unleaded gas. Top up at half a tank and don't worry. In fact, along the border — from Tijuana to Matamoros —the gas you buy was imported from the U.S.

Only 2 1/2 hours south, stop in **San Fernando**. Across from the Pemex station with unleaded gas is an unexpected jewel. At the cafe by the **Motel Hacienda**, you might meet Henry Kowalski, the owner, if he's not guiding hunters. If he asks you, with his eyes downcast, "Do you play a little chess?", you'd better tell the truth.

I admitted that I played, "a little". Henry is a few points shy of holding a master rating. Sometimes arrogant people will overstate their abilities and Henry has to trounce them.

He recalled one gringo who played poorly until they put money on the games. Then he whipped up on him — reckon he was a Texas boy, don't you?

47

Henry told me of one other chess player who'd travelled that highway. A Mercedes pulled up one day. A young woman drove. She and another woman helped the man in the back get out and into a wheelchair. They were tall and gorgeous. The trio had stopped for some of Henry's soup (which you should too). They go to talking, as travellers will do.

The man was a painter, a famous one, on his way to Mexico City for a showing of his work. Since he was paraplegic, and could only move his head, Henry assumed (as did I) that he painted with a brush in his teeth. The they played chess. Then Henry learned that you can't assume anything in this life.

The painter beat Henry in a few moves. Henry was shocked. The old man laughed.

"Son, I had you beat in 3 moves. I'd already played the whole game in my head."

Henry shook his head.

"How do you think I paint?"

"I assume, señor, that you have a brush between your teeth."

The painter laughed. "In my head, ... it's all in my head. You see these beautiful young girls?" He nodded his head right, then left. "All you see is the outside. They are more than beautiful women, they are my arms, my hands. I paint the picture in my head, then tell them what strokes to make. Their beauty comes from inside and I help them share it with the world."

Dusk had closed on the cafe when Henry finished that story. The only sounds were the distant traffic and the whirring of the ceiling fan. I thanked Henry and left. That night I slept well. Stories like that are rare, and I was honored to have been given one. Stories like that only come from roadside cafes, comfort stops on highways to somewhere else.

You can extol the advantages of flying all you want, but stories like that only come from roadside cafes, comfort stops on highways to somewhere else.

You'd expect flat, dull marshlands. There's about 160 miles of unbroken flat, but no marsh. Then, like a desert mirage, a small mountain range materializes. Those are the Rusias (Russians). After miles of nothing (kinda like South Texas), the road slices through the bellies of white-limestone hills. You'd think it was the Ozarks. Little towns appear like magic kingdoms, then recede as you fall southward.

Abruptly, the hills disappear as suddenly as they arose and you flatland it into **Tampico**. About 30 miles north, you pass a Pemex with unleaded gas and lady attendants. Yep, it's a growing trend. One of them told me her boss preferred women since they were more courteous and honest than men. I wouldn't dare comment on that.

Just before **Altamira**, four lane divided begins and the pace of the traffic picks up. The controlled anarchy that is driving in Mexican cities takes over. If you let it take you over, allow yourself to flow with the traffic, you'll learn to love

48

it. If you don't, it'll beat you down. Not too far beyond is a fancy RV park on a lake and golf course — **Miralta's.**

Seaports are busy, and industrious in daylight. Everybody seems to be working, or thinking about it. After sunset, the city shows its inner self. With two plazas to choose from, you'll can enjoy real folks being real Mexicans. Forget floor shows and troopes of folks who get paid to help you forget home. For free, the friendly folks in Tampico will make you feel as if you haven't a care in the world.

The blackbirds and I prefer the Plaza de la Libertad about sunset. They're attracted to the shade trees. The "bird man of Tampico" is attracted by them.

I talked to the interesting old fellow several times, but we couldn't agree on just one name for him. A proud, only slightly bent, white-haired, impeccable mustachioed man of 60 to 90, he's a living scarecrow.

Funereally clad in a black coat, pants and hat, he'll chat with you about several subjects at once, smiling. Once a nearby tree fills with too many birds for his taste, he forgets you. He'll dash off, **WHAP, WHAP**, the tree and shout at the birds. They'll leave. He'll stand there, shaking his fist at them. Then he'll turn and triumphantly stride over to another tree and start talking up a storm. He was just as happy to talk to the tree as to me. That happens to me a lot. I couldn't discover why he did what he did, but only know that he did it well.

Across from the bird plaza is one of the largest hardware stores I've ever seen — one-half a city block wide and just as deep. But, urban hardware junkies, don't get your hopes up! I went in to browse and discovered that it's no serve yourself shop. The good stuff is off-limits. They supply the nearby farmers and smaller "ferreterias" with goods. Since UHJ's like me often don't know the names of the stuff we cart home from hardware stores at home, I was lost there. I bought some batteries to save face and slinked out.

The other plaza, the Plaza de Armas is the eating plaza. Liquado and fruit stands anchor two of the corners. One of them is shaped (pretty much) like a streetcar. No one has a key for it, so it's open 24 hours.

A liquado is Mexico's greatest bargain. It's like a smoothie, only better. Papaya, melon or anything else that grows nearby is cut, chopped and liquefied with milk, cinnamon, sugar or honey, yogurt or eggs or .... in a blender and served in an old-fashioned malted milk glass.

The **Inglaterra** (PH: 12-5678) is the Grand Dame of town, anchoring the square with her stolid quality. Surprisingly, this 5 story Grand Hotel escapes the ticky-tacky atmosphere of most modern first-class places. She has an elegance, like an new sailing ship built in the traditional style. Sometimes there'll be specials that make her economical.

A double runs from $25-$60, depending the day. Ask.

The **Colonial** (PH: 2-7676) is interesting. The lobby with hanging plants, carpet and small tables at the video bar belie her age. The owner is a young fellow which has some respect for tradition. Parking is at a garage across the street. Doubles are $30-$40.

The **Impala** (PH: 12-0990, 12-0684) is an interesting place, 4 stories, 80 rooms and some atmosphere. While it's not as fancy as the Inglaterra, it **feels** far more comfortable. It's a solid, middle-class place. Rooms are carpeted and quiet. I liked it. The staff seems friendly, which is a big plus in my book. Rooms run $18-25, which is OK, but Sanborn's Mexico Club members get an additional 20% off.

The **Regis** is the oldest hotel in town and a bit cheaper. I'd like to recommend the Monte Carlo, because the place is downtown, quiet and nice — but the surly help there can ruin a stay.

Budget-wise, the **Tampico** (PH: 12-4970) is one of those "faded elegance" places that some of us love. An OK room will only set you back about $10-$15.

Nearby is the **Cafe Mundo** (note it's not "el" Mundo, just "Mundo"). Every town has one. It's the "City Diner" of yesteryear. Students, office workers and old-timers stream in and out 24 hours a day. The tables wobble, the tablecloths don't match and the windows don't get cleaned very often. The three waiters seem to be there all the time, which is hard to believe, since they look like ush-ers at a funeral parlor. Still, it's my kind of place and the food's cheap and good. Breakfast'll run $1.20—$2.00, lunch $1.75—$3.00.

Seafood is the champ here, but the main contenders are two unique restaurants, back to back. **Diligencias** is the winner for its huge portions, variety (over 200 styles of seafood) and taste. A meal there will set you back about $20 for two. Sr. **Miguel Angel Castillo**, (PH: 12-2668, 12-0007) of Tamaulipas Department of Tourism recommended the place and I'm in his debt. It was the best seafood I've ever had. The outside might put you off, since it does look plain, maybe even seedy. But, like many things Mexican, there's always something beneath the surface. The inner room is a white-tablecloth area.

Saloon Palacio is the sort of place Jack London used to hang out. It's been cleaned up, but the atmosphere's there. Everywhere you look, there's a reminder that this is no Howard Johnson's. The floor is marble and you'll see relics everywhere you look — a few real marble tables and some plastic marble ones, sea-chests hanging from the rafters, left there by those multi-nationalitied men who ply their wares on the waves, a wooden mermaid who once cut the waves of the seas. The waiters are characters, too.

Now that you've been bedded and fed, you'll want to see the sea.

Here's the big surprise: Tampico has a gorgeous beach, as pretty as South Padre Island used to be fore so many condos sprouted, and the sand is virgin-white!

Getting there is a bit tricky, but if you follow Tampico's "Tourist Route" signs (a white palm tree on a brilliant blue background), you'll make it. Go through the Pemex refinery in **Cd. Madero** until the road dead ends. Then you can either turn left on a hard-sand, sometimes asphalt road, or drive into the ocean. You won't find your view blocked by sun-blocking high-rises — not today, anyway.

Play to your heart's content on the miles of unpopulated beach, cool off in the sinfully warm (60-72 degree F.) water and enjoy while you can. "Development" is planned. Good for tourism, but can they present us with a place that preserves some Mexican flavor and not another Cancún?

There are seafood eateries galore and one good restaurant on the hill as you hit the beach.

I remembered this beach from several years before, after an oil spill had blackened everything. Time heals wounds and cleans beaches. If you were there before, you'll be impressed.

From here, you can keep going South to the delightful river-port, volcanic sand beaches of **Tuxpan** in 6 hours, on you way to Veracruz (about 4 hours more), the Yucatan a day further or finally the Caribbean, about 2 days from Veracruz.

West, you'll run into **Valles**, once a booming tourist "destination" and now a progressive, laid-back town. If you stay there, the **Hotel Posada Don Antonio** is the best deal in town and the old sulphur-spring resort of **Tanninul**, where the likes of Burt Lancaster and his cronies used to party. A couple of hours south of there is **Xilitla**, where an eccentric Englishman built a castle and ground of Dalí-esque sculptures amid an orchid forest. South of there and you'll bump into the mountains and orchid forests in a few hours. Aim northwest towrds home and soak up the part-colonial, part-modern charm of Victoria in 6 hours.

No matter how you go, you'll be rewarded with lustrous little-known jewels. Leave the more advertised spots to those who don't know any better. We'll take the jewels over the dross.

This page left intentionally blank.

NOTES

Pto. Vallarta Hotels

Sunday, November 18, 1990

If you're not lucky enough to get a jacuzzi in your room, the **Molino de Agua** (Aptdo 54, Puerto Vallarta, Jal. PH: (322) 2-1907, 2-1957) has one of the best big ones in Mexico.

It's unique. Perched just over the bridge over the Río Cuale, it's in the old section of town. The Río Cuale is the dividing line between the old and the new, or at least it used to be. Now it's the line between the fun and sun airhead kind of tourist and the other kind.

I'm not sure what the other kind is, but I'm one of 'em. It's not about money; it's about attitude. I've met rich folks at fancy hotels who are more *simpático* than many of the backpackers who've travelled much but learned little.

The **Molino** is family-run. The *dueña* is a sharp business-woman who hovers over everything to make sure things are done right. She has weekly staff meetings and explains that if the tourists aren't happy, they won't come back and nobody'll have a job. She wouldn't let me take her picture, saying she's like a movie star — she'd prefer to keep the memories of when she was young and beautiful. Beauty comes in different forms and she'll always be beautiful.

The hotel is a tropical garden in an urban setting. There are three types of rooms — cottages, duplex cottages and three storied suites on the beach. All are quiet. **Parking** is **ample** and **secure.**

Meander to your cottage on a stone path. Pass some arrogant parrots and a cocky monkey who'll snatch your glasses if you let him lure you too close. Then read the sign warning you in English, Spanish and French. The restaurant is in a thatched-roof, South Seas palapa at the edge of one of the pools.

Opposite is the **jacuzzi. And what a jacuzzi it is!** It's set into a rock grotto, has rock and plaster walls, and is deep enough to stand up. It's roomy. I've shared it with eight other bubble-water worshipers and none of us was close enough to raise even the most conservative eyebrow.

Some of you may think I've got the skin of an old toad and webbed feet from the way I carry on about water. It's not true. My feet are not webbed!

The rooms are pleasant and the ample suites have rough-rock floors and beds set into seashell (that seems to be the trend in fancy-dancy places, too). They all overlook the beach, and you can leave your windows open at night.

If you're like me, you'll prefer the sound of crashing surf to the humming of the air-conditioning. Of course, the *señora* is proud of the A/C, so be sure she doesn't catch you. She'll rush up to see why it isn't working. Like I said, she does

53

everything she can to make sure you're comfortable.

If you're lucky, you're not very much like me. I tote a white noise machine that imitates the surf — just in case I wake up in Chihuahua.

The best thing about the Molino is the price. It'll only set you back about $35-60, depending on your room.

§§§§§§§§§§§§§§§§§§§§§

An interviewer told me today that one of the most popular RV destinations is now Creel, Chih. He asked why Creel had leaped to the top of the chart. Even as modest as I am, I have to take a little credit. Honest as I am, I can't take all of it.

Bill & Joyce Holmberg, who run **Aztec Custom RV Tours** (P.O. Box 1478, Aztec NM 87410 **PH: 800-962-6073**), told me about Creel. They're tall folks, in many ways, and about three years ago, Bill opened the Copper Canyon for me, describing the then new road between Cuahutemoc & Creel with such fervor that I logged it for Sanborn's, then began talking it up. I know other folks promoted it, but it's nice to think that he and I had a small part in helping tourism there.

They have a caravan leaving for **Colonial Mexico** on **Dec. 21**; another for the Yucatan on **Jan. 13**.

Another interesting fellow who runs his own tours is **Norm Yelland. (Caravans Mexico & Central America**, 1129 Minnesota Ave., Brownsville, Tx 78521. PH: (512) **831-6190**.). Norm's a big man, too, but not in height. He and his son **Chris** are experts on **Guatemala**. They live there most of the year. Norm likes to keep things simple and he's so independent that he attracts independent caravaners.

He's doing a **Mexico East Coast, Belize and Guatemala RV** tour leaving **Jan. 6th**. Some days they only cover 8 miles! If you want to go beyond Mexico, he's your man. Hurry, though — he won't take over 13 units. I think it's because he doesn't want to work hard, but he say's it's because folks enjoy themselves better.

§§§§§§§§§§§§§§§§§§§§§

"Mexico" Mike doesn't think very much — it gives him a headache. Although his feet are more normal than he, it's still difficult to write Sanborn's Travelog with webbed fingers.

54

Copper Canyon 2

Sunday, November 25, 1990

Folks, I didn't mean to leave you hanging in the Copper Canyon. Ol' Mike has short-term memory loss sometimes.

We got as far as Cuauhtemoc last time, so here's the rest of the trip. Leaving Cuauhtemoc, the road changes from rolling hills to twisty mountain drives. Turn left at a tumble-down shack on the left.

Two-lane, but well-paved the road climbs through the prairie. A Mexicanism (something that operates just a little bit differently South of the Border) occurs. This wonderful road dead ends as it comes to the town of **San Juanito**. It re-appears at the other end. What happened is that there was a political squabble between fathers and the highway department, so they skipped the town when paving.

Go slow. It's cobblestone and gravel. If it's late in the day, stop in at **Motel Posada del Cobre**, a wonderful, charming oasis at the north entrance to town. The restaurant attached is plain and wholesome and the rooms which cost $22 are comfy. Some have fireplaces.

Only 2 miles more and you come to a series of "S" curves that demand you take it easy. Eight miles farther, a stone Jesus greets you with outstretched hands. Boy, was I glad to see Him!

At the top of the hill, turn left to get to hotels. The **Parador de la Montaña** (145-6-0075 or 6-0085) is

the nicest, has spot for self-contained RV's to park and has the best restaurant in town with continental meals. If you go straight, you'll come to the hotel on the edge of the Canyon. We describe it as "rustic". The **Copper Canyon Lodge** is the oldest lodge in the area. It's rustic, has fireplaces and attracts Europeans.

You can hike from the **Cusarare Waterfall**. In an hour or so, you'll be sitting on the edge of a precipice and wonder about it all. There's a stillness and an elegant majesty there that calms your nerves and takes you out of yourself. That's why you came isn't it?

Your hotel can arrange a tour to go to the bottom of the canyon where legend has it that there are hidden hunks of silver the size of basketballs. At the bottom, the contrast of semi-tropical vegetation and Alpine-like mountains may make you ask what's "normal". That's the kind of place it is.

It's not the same effect as the **Grand Canyon**. Although grander in scale than the Arizona wonder, this canyon's greatness is in its contrasts — not its colors. The Grand Canyon's surreal — the Copper Canyon's magical.

There aren't many places to eat, but the restaurant **Gran Vision**, run by the lovely Rita is good at a fair price. Just past the top of the hill, across from the Pemex station.

If you want to "do" the Canyon, leave your vehicle at your hotel and take the train to Los Mochis. You can do it in a day and return the next. It has English-speaking lady guides who'll tell you what you're passing.

The railroad was the dream of an American dreamer, Albert Kimsey Owens, who in 1872, had a vision of a railroad connecting the American East with California by way of Chihuahua, the Copper Canyon, Topolobombo, "place of the land turtles" and ocean freighters. He convinced dozens of middle-class Americans to emigrate with their families to Topolobombo to further his dream. There are decedants of Kinsey's "American Colony" in Topo.

After him, there several attempts to link East and West, but the land was tougher than the men. In 1961 the final track was laid. There are 38 bridges and 86 tunnels between Chihuahua and Los Mochis.

When its time to return take a left just before Cuauhtemoc and return to El Paso (or Douglas) by the scenic route through Mennonite country. Pass up the "Hotel California" in San Buenavena. If you come or go by way of Douglas, Arizona, stop in Bisbee, an old mining town. Stay at the bed & breakfast, **The Inn at Castle Rock**, one half mile down Tombstone Canyon Road. Rates $35-45 double. All rooms are unique and include breakfast. This is where you'll meet fellow travellers like yourself.

The owner, Jim Babcock, **walked** the Copper Canyon before there were roads or railroads. A geologist, he's an old Mexican who has lived to share his knowledge with the rest of us. It's folks like him that make us Mexico travellers a unique breed. We always find each other — in McAllen, Texas or Bisbee, Arizona.

56

Cd. Victoria

Sunday, December 2, 1990

The highlight of my visit to Cd. Victoria, Tamps. was not getting into prison. It was getting out. That trip, I learned about freedom, fear and miracles.

I've had more than a passing acquaintance with jails — Mexican and U.S. Of course that was long ago in my checkered past. Some ghosts die hard, and that awful sensation that creeps up my legs and slithers into my heart when I hear an iron door creak-clang-shut behind me, reawakened an old one. You only have to be on the wrong end of one of those gates once to dislike it intensely.

Of course, there are other things to do in Cd. Victoria, lots of 'em. In fact, the place has so much to offer that it's one of my favorite cities. Since I've been to most of 'em, my vote's worth something. It's only 702 KM from Mexico City and a mere 320 KM from McAllen or Brownsville.

Lots of towns are named Ciudad (Cd. for short), and it doesn't have anything to do with their size. Some are known as Cd. by everybody. Some are called that only on special days and by the city fathers. I'd explain the reason behind this, but I don't understand it. It's a Mexicanism. That's a phrase I borrowed from Ed Gill for things that operate in Mexico without rhyme or reason. Believe me, you'll enjoy yourself a lot more if you just assign most of the things you can't explain to the Mexicanism category.

Cd. Victoria sits at the foothills of the deceptively friendly-looking Sierra Madre mountains, at 900 feet above sea level. The Sierra Gorda mountain dominates the town. About 250,000 folks call it home, and most of 'em are pretty friendly. You can walk around town day or night without fear of being assaulted, unlike some towns of the same size on both sides of the border. The climate's pretty darn nice in the winter — it has few days with temperatures in the 30's F. January and the spring and fall are okey-dokey, too. Summer can be a tad hot, unless you're from south Texas, in which case, they'll have to heat up hell for you. You folks from big cities will appreciate the air. Although you can't see it, it's mighty breathable. There's little smoke-stack industry, and there aren't too many cars — yet.

In fact that's one of the chief attractions of it for people who haven't driven in Mexico a lot. The traffics's civilized and polite. There are lots of stoplights that work and people don't feel they have to blast you into motion the moment the red light flows into green.

Many of the people who live there are still employed in agriculture. There's lots of cattle ranching around and citrus is grown nearby. The most noticeable are the Mennonites who live a non-mechanized

57

existence and ride into town in horse-driven buggies to sell their cheeses and other farm products. Many folks think the Mennonites are found only in Chihuahua, and there are lots there, but a few wandered all about Mexico.

They're interesting people. They were pushed from one place to the next in the U.S. because of their religious beliefs. When they were pushed to the Rio Grande (actually, the Mexican border, since the Rio Grande doesn't run the full length of it), they had to come to Mexico. They made a deal with the government — "we won't get involved in politics and will work hard, be industrious and pay taxes if you just let us alone." The deal sounded good to both. They've pretty much kept their word. Mexico's a strange place, and many a strange bed-partner is made here.

Mick Jagger would love them, since their favorite color is black.

Everybody wears black clothes. The women favor black dresses, though their bonnet may have some color (a woman is a woman, Mennonite or not). The men cover themselves with black coats, black pants and white shirts. They favor a large-brimmed flat black hat. They're not unfriendly, but they are reserved. They're noted for hygienic food preparation, so their foodstuffs (particularly cheeses) are sought after.

Lots of other Victorians are employed by the government, since this is the capital of Tamaulipas. Most of these offices are located in a modern steel and glass highrise on the edge of the city.

Downtown are the old government buildings and the city administration. You can take a walking tour of them with ease. Just point your nose at the north end of the Plaza de Armas, facing the cinema. Go two blocks, take a right and you'll be wandering around the halls of Tamaulipas history. The government palace with its murals is 7 blocks west.

The cinema is like the rest of Cd. Victoria — there's more to it than meets the eye. Outside, it's a normal, modern-looking movie-house, where you might see Rambo or Bambi, depending on your taste. Inside, though, is a pretty neat mural, depicting the founding of Cd. Victoria. It runs the whole length of the building, on the wall behind the popcorn and candy concession. It depicts the settling of the land by the Huasteca Indians, to the Spanish conquest, and of course, the Revolution.

Next week we'll visit more of the city and experience a miracle. The Prison story I've saved for last.

$$$$$$$$$$$$$$$$$$$$$$$$$

"Mexico" Mike is on the road again, off to Baja California. He said he's looking for a white whale or something.

Cd. Victoria: Miracle

Sunday, December 9, 1990

I got my second fan letter before I left. Gee, thanks for the kind words. I won't let it swell my head, but don't stop. Now we know there are at least two readers out there! I also got a less than fan letter from AAA. Humm, I wonder who put a bee in their bonnet? I thank them for writing, too. When I get back, I'll respond and let you know if we're able to work things out. They said they want to promote Mexico, sort of. They said I didn't. It should be interesting, folks.

There's a lot more to Cd. Victoria than meets the eye! Let's see what we can see. There's a small, but interesting and informative historical and anthropological museum behind the theater. There's no one around to explain things to you in English, but if you read Spanish you'll enjoy it. Heck, I enjoyed places like that better when I could just pick out a word here and there. History's fine, but I like romance a lot better.

The state university is about a mile from the city center. It boasts a number of fairly modern buildings, fountains and some pretty grounds. Again, there's a wonderful mural inside the building. It goes up the staircase and ends on the ceiling. I've had nights like that, too. If you're like me (poor thing), then you'll enjoy just sitting around the ample plaza and watch local folks doing what they do best — being themselves. In fact, that's one of the things that attracted *Norteamericanos* south in the first place, but they seldom take the time to enjoy. Do it. Folks promenade around the square, sit on the benches as the sun sets and visit. It's a return to a way and pace of life that could do all of us urbanites some good.

Okay, that may not be excitement enough for all of you. How about a combination shrine to the Virgin and waterfall? Drive north on Hwy #85, and a bit west for one hour to *El Chorrito* — the only place where I experienced a miracle.

The story is the Virgin Mary appeared in a cave here. The Catholic Church built a church at the site, incorporating the cave into the rear wall, by the altar. I kind of like the idea of a rock cave projecting into a plain vanilla church.

Behind the church was the passageway to the sacred spot. Sure enough, there was a mound of crutches at the entrance, mute testaments to the efficacy of the healing power of the Virgin of *Chorrito*. In the middle of the cave was the exact spot where the Virgin appeared. As we got to the end of the walkway through the cave, and prepared to come out the other side, I stopped to examine the objects stuck in the pockmarked rock wall. There were pictures and cameos of young men, old men, girls, boys, women and pets that people had placed there to pray for.

The hunchback grabbed me. Then he grabbed my camera. His face was frozen in a death mask-like grin. I lost my voice. My friends had already left the cave, so it was just me, the hunchback and the ghosts of those who'd asked the Virgin to intercede. I started to pray myself.

When we assume the obvious, we're usually wrong. The unfortunate-looking fellow was simply trying to get me to take a picture of the wall before I left. It should not have come out at all, since I was shooting ASA 100 film in a cave illuminated by 40 watt bulbs. Of course, my flash had long ago died.

I wasn't about to disappoint him, so I shot away. When I had them developed, they came out! They weren't bright enough to reproduce here, but they were visible, though a little dark. Some people believe that the energy from the cave made the images on the film. Others get real silent and nod their heads in awe. Those folks think the Virgin did it. Me, I don't know.

§§§§§§§§§§§§§§§§§§§§§§

"Mexico" Mike hasn't reported in from the Baja yet. He says he has a job updating Sanborn's Travelog, but we think he's a spy. We just can't figure out for what country. If he's in town, you can reach him at Sanborn's Mexico Insurance office, 2009 S. 10th, or care of this paper, but we can't figure out why you'd want to.

Prison Life

Sunday, December 16, 1990

Okay, folks, I know you're ready to see me go to prison. I know AAA is. You didn't think I'd leave you in the cave, did you? After the cave, head on up the road a piece and you'll come to the falls known as *El Chorrito*. They're not the biggest in the world, but they're mighty pretty. The water's clear, cold and clean.

One of the things that makes Mexico is what it is the humble, unaffected people who run little businesses tucked away in small towns. A business like this is run by a family right by the falls. They sell cold drinks to folks who can picnic by the stream that runs down the little hill there. You can swim in the ponds that the stream pauses in before it winds it's way on down towards Cd. Victoria. It's simple, pastoral and really Mexican. I can't think of a better way to spend an afternoon.

On the way back, you'll pass old sugar haciendas, with their aqueducts that still carry water to people who live nearby. We stopped at one little home where a family made piloncillo (sugar candy) the old-fashioned way. The sugar cane is fed into a cone, then pushed down into the iron roller that will squeeze the juice out of the cane. Sometimes the press is turned by hand, other times by a trusty burro. Sadly, the harvest was bad this year so the folks who fed me my cane sugar treat weren't doing well. If you do stop, these folks will be glad to demonstrate the old process, but the polite thing to do is to buy a piece of candy for a few dollars.

Oh, I wasn't really a prisoner. I was just visiting. The prisoners make really nice furniture from ebony, cypress and pine. It's an interesting deal, real free (well as free as it can be from behind bars) enterprise. One prisoner buys the wood and owns the lathes etc. Some prisoners work for him, others use the machinery for their personal works of art. The prisoners put their name on the pieces they make. When one of them sells, the money is credited to them, less what they owe for materials. I got to visit the cellblock itself, where the prisoners had made things quite cozy. One fellow was softly strumming a guitar, a few were playing cards and one was reading a novella. Most of the cells had privacy, with cardboard cartons covering the bars. There were connubial visits.

In the corner was a little kitchen, where the prisoners could buy their meals. In a Mexican prison, if you don't have family, you'd better be able to buy food. The state does provide a minimal diet, but don't count on getting fat on it. The slops are fed to hogs that roam the grounds outside. Don't be out there when it's slopping time. I was and the guards get a little edgy. I was too as a file of felons rushed by me, carrying buckets of aromatic hog food. The guards with their rifles at

61

the ready position didn't help any, either. I felt more comfortable when Mateo, my guide was near me. At the end of the trip, I bought a couple of items, as a gesture of friendship. One of them he'd made. He was a young kid, 20 years old. I asked why he was there. "I murdered three students", he smiled. "Oh!" He smiled broadly. "Don't worry, I was young — only 16 and I was drunk." "I hope you don't get drunk anymore." "No, not like that. I am older now and can handle my liquor." As I strolled back to my car under the checkerboard shade from the ancient trees lining the driveway, I was reflective.

Life in Mexico is like a duck paddling on a still pond. On the surface all was serene, but underneath she was paddling like hell. No matter how long I stayed here, no matter how often I returned, I'd never understand her. Beneath the surface all is different, all is beyond logic. !Viva Mexico! GUIDE: **Candelario Chico Amoro**, Las Adelitas #166 PH: 6-2219, or ask for him at the Sierra Gorda. LODGING: The **Hotel Sierra Gorda**, Av. Hidalgo Ote. #990, PH: (131) 2-2010, FAX: 2-9799 is reasonable, quiet and a wonderful place to stay.

Durango — Mechanic

Christmas. Durango. Hotel Gobernador. Car no go. No worry. On road too long. I don't care. Another day, or week, doesn't matter.

In Mexico things always work out, but not always the way you expect. I'm thankful the car made it over the "Devil's Backbone" (*el Espinazo del Diablo*) from Mazatlán.

The problem appears minor — a clogged fuel filter. No mechanical problem is minor for me, so I'm prepared for anything.

I don't bother to ask at the front desk for a mechanic. Experience tells me the desk clerk (or manager) would smile brightly as he gave me directions to the Chevy dealer, then sadly shake his head as he remembered it's Christmas Day. He'd only be doing what he'd been taught tourists want to hear.

Roadies like you and me know better. Mexican mechanics are one of their national treasures. They can fix things with few or no parts, or make the ones they need.

I lifted the hood to attract the guardia of the parking lot. I do better with mechanics (often called *maestros*) in Mexico than in the U.S. There I'm not worried about losing my dignity or appearing unmanly.

I'm just a "dumb gringo," so it's okay if I don't know exactly why the darn thing won't work. It's kind of like being "just a woman" here. It frees me from a lot of stress.

The guard nods wisely as I say I think it's the *filtro sucio* (dirty filter) that's the problem. Of course, he doesn't do that sort of work, but he has a friend who does. Of course, in only fifteen minutes, everything will be hunky-dory. Mexicans are often optimistic about time, so I agree, but don't count on it.

After about twenty minutes, I return to see how it's going. By golly, there's a young guy there, Alejandro, and he's working away, though he has a pained look on his face. The filter requires two wrenches of the same size. He has a very mismatched set of tools that doesn't have two of anything the same.

We're in luck. I have a good set of Buffalo wrenches. The filter won't budge, but he can remove another long piece of fuel line, take the filter to another friend who has a vise and then they can get it off. Makes perfect sense to me. Maybe I've become Mexican.

In less than an hour the operation is done. The proud surgeon stands back from his patient and grins. I pretend to inspect. We stand together with the cold Durango wind at our backs and the warm Chevy eight cylinders roaring at us.

Alejandro guides my fingers under the filter to show me that there's no gas leaking. The filter's so cold from the gas that it's hard to touch. He instinctively understands,

63

gets a white cloth and puts it under the seals. No leaks. I nod and act satisfied. I shake his hand and tell him I'm impressed. I am, too.

Time has come to pay. I know that nobody's going to come out on a freezing cold Christmas Day for free. Before I ask Alejandro what he wants, I look at the shiny matched set of wrenches he's putting back into their plastic case. He handles them with as much care and respect as if they were made of bone china.

He hands them slowly to me, eyes downcast.

"Le gusta?" I ask. (Do you like them?)

"Si! Muy fina." (Oh yes! They are very fine, nice, good.)

My friends have never accused me of terminal generosity, but I knew then that the wrenches would be in better hands in Durango than in mine anywhere. I hand them to him.

"Un regalo," I say. (A gift.) I knew I didn't have to but then I ask what he will charge for his work. He tells me to buy the guardia a coffee. I do better than that.

Back in my room, I ran a steaming bath and unpacked my portable jacuzzi. I settled into my bubbles and sighed, "Ho, ho, ho."

Giving does feel good. As always, things worked out in the Mexican way. I made a friend, learned something about myself and had a warm place to sleep. It was a good Christmas.

The **Gobernador-Presidente**, Av. 20 de Noviembre #257, PH:

(181) 3-1919, FAX (181) 1-1422, is one of my favorite hotels. It's a converted monastery. The Hollywood folk stay there when filming in Durango, but I like it anyway. A double costs about $70-80, the rooms are quiet and they have tubs, so bring your jacuzzi!

Next week, I'll tell you about a lady who touched my calloused old heart. **Susana Eger Valadez** runs the *Huichol* (Indian) *Center* in **Santiago Ixcuintla, Nayarit** & has one of the most touching stories I've heard. She's one of the people who are truly making a difference in the world. While you and I are just living, she's quietly saving people's lives and a whole tribe's way of life. I felt truly humble in her presence. I hope you'll read her story next week.

"Mexico" Mike was lost in the ozone for a month, but unfortunately found his way home. As usual, he was gone too long and got lost, but he did update Sanborn's Travelog in Baja.

Huichol

Sunday, January 13, 1991

This is a love story. Like love, it's both uplifting and sad. You'll write the end. I only do beginnings.

I'm not a parent. That's good, I think. But it took a parent to explain why I care, why we can all care about a group of Indians called **Huichols**.

They live in Nayarit state. They're dying faster than they're living. They create eyesocket-shocking artwork that burns itself into your soul with bright blues, yellows and fierce reds in beadwork, yarn weavings, & more.

I'm no art critic. Nobody accuses me of being sensitive. W.C. Fields and I have similar views on children and dogs.

Even the meanest S.O.B. in the Valley, would know he was in the presence of something warm, kind and gentle if he met a Huichol.

Julio Birrueta, convention manager of **El Cid Resort (PH: (678) 3-3333, USA 1-800-525-1925)** in **Mazatlán** explained it to me.

We were talking business when I felt an inner urging to open up to him — a feeling that disrupts what I think I want to do and pushes in a new direction.

I heard myself telling him about my visit to the **Huichol Center for Cultural Survival** in Santiago **Ixcuintla, Nayarit**. It's 146.5 miles south, then 8 KM west on Hwy #15, of Mazatlán.

"*Si*," he said "I have seen them. They are very *orgulloso* (proud) people."

"They need somebody to care. The infant mortality rate is 50%."

His stern businessman's face dropped.

"Cincuenta! You mean one out of two babies dies?"

"Yeah. **TB epidemic. Malnutrition. Famine.** No clean drinking water." I felt hopeless just telling him. Can you imagine being a parent there?

Julio looked beyond me and into the deepening twilight that crept into his office.

"I'm a father," he said simply. "And I am a man. If I lose my arm, I will find a way to feed myself. But a child cannot take care of himself. *We must protect the children.* If not, we cannot call ourselves men, or human beings."

Talk's cheap. Action speaks. He's inviting them for an exhibition at El Cid.

Susana Eger Valadez, and her Huichol husband Mariano, hold the center together.

She laughs often. Her voice is like her: sweetly alive, filled with hope, comforting, sincere.

"We're here because they come to work the crops six months out of the year. When they get...sick from the contagious diseases most of us are immunized for, it's disastrous...especially if they go back to their homeland and contaminate the rest of the tribe. We're trying to put a brake on the medical problems."

The Center is a two story dark sand-colored house on the main street, across from a funeral parlor with a coffin above a beer sign.

"We are supported through the sale of artwork. There are no fees." No bleeding-heart pushover, she adds, "My condition is that no one be idle while they're here recuperating. The idea is to give them self-respect and pride in their work and their heritage."

As migrants, they aren't treated at local hospitals. Their shamans admit there are "outsider's diseases" they can't treat. They combine traditional healing (herbs, prayer, shamans) and the miracles of modern men of medicine.

She came 20 years ago to get an anthropology doctorate. Now she's raising consciousness and children. There are some things more important than degrees, though she got it later.

She fell in love, with a man, with a people.

An Indian teacher, J. Krishnamurti writes better than I: "When you see a sharp stone on a path trodden by many bare feet, you remove it, not because you have been asked but because you feel for another...you may never meet. Without love there is no freedom; without love, freedom is merely an idea that has no value...."

On the way out, we went through Susana & Mariano's bedroom.

"Nice VCR", I said though I saw no TV. In fact, I didn't see much at all, except a bed that sagged as much as my spirits on a **really** bad day.

"Yes," Susana said her voice only a little less cheerful than usual, "I'll miss it. We have to sell it to pay the food bill."

I'm not the smartest guy to come from Edinburg HS, but I didn't ask about the TV.

I did what little I could to help. Not much. I bought something beautiful, but it pales compared to what she and the Huichols gave me.

To get a color catalog of their work; give a few dollars or invite them for an exhibition, write: **Huichol Center, P.O. Box 1430, Cottonwood, AZ 86326. PH: (602) 634-3946**. Make checks to "Huichol Center."

"Mexico" Mike recovered from his bout of kindness & was seen kicking a dog on his way to work at Sanborn's, where he writes their Mexico highway guide, The Travelog.

66

Shortcuts

Sunday, January 20, 1991

Shortcuts often aren't. The last one I took turned out to be the road that wasn't.

It's not hard to be humble when my memory works. 'Course I have a built-in forgetter that enables me to ignore those times when I was less than perfect — like the time I took the cutup shortcut.

I reckon lots of y'all are like me when it comes to maps. You stare at them, imagining the adventures that await you at each unknown dot.

Most folks have better sense than to let that dominate their lives, but I was absent the day they taught common sense. That's why I'm a roadlogger instead of somebody with a respectable job.

From Real de Catorce to Zacatecas should be an easy drive. You can go via San Tiburcio and Hwy #54, or Hwy #57, Matehuala to San Luis Potosi, then west on Hwy #49.

I didn't do either. Sadly, there were a couple of folks with me who were fooled into thinking I knew what I was doing.

Don't you ever get the urge to blaze a new trail?

"But Mike," Trusting Soul #1 asked at the first crossroads, "it's shorter to go to Hwy #54."

"Yeah," I said and turned right towards Hwy #57. I'm not big on explanations.

There was an ominous silence, so I tried a diversion.

"Look! On the right — doesn't that mountain look like the one in *The Treasure of the Sierra Madre*?"

My former friends stared at some vague mountain. After all, they were with the illustrious "Mexico Mike".

We rolled through Matehuala without incident. (By the way there's a new hotel there, more next week).

"Where exactly is this turnoff to your shortcut," Trusting Soul #2 (from now on abbreviated TS) asked.

"I'm not sure."

I kept my eyes on the road, but I **knew** they had that look.

"I thought you'd been everywhere," TS#1 said.

"Nobody's been everywhere. That's why I took this vacation."

Hah, I thought, let 'em mull that over! I kept driving.

Luckily, a gasoline truck decided to pass a cattle truck on the two lane road just then. Naturally, I followed hard on his bumper.

I figured anybody with good sense would get out of the way.

I was wrong. You should have seen the look on that VW driver's face when the gas jockey whipped in front of the cattle truck. There we were, a surprise!

I saw two scenarios. #1 — the VW **might** brake, the gas truck **speed up** and the bovine carrier **slow down** so I could get in; #2 — we'd all die.

I know there's a gasoline truck with my name on it out there, but that wasn't it.

The VW politely ran off the road to avoid getting to know us better.

Burning rubber smell assaulted our noses, screaming air brakes filled our ears, adrenalin flooded our bodies. God help me, I love it so. Three collective gasps sucked in air.

Quiet reigned for the next few miles. Before distrust could re-erupt, we topped a rise and saw a sign for "Charcas".

"Aha!" I shouted.

"Another gas truck!" TS#1 screamed.

"Where?" I screamed and hit the brakes.

"Jesus save us!" TS#2 prayed and hit the floorboard.

When we all stopped shaking, I turned right. The road was great! Two lane blacktop. Shoulders. Road signs. Tensions dropped. We sang a song as we rolled along.

Charcas is a pleasant little town. We bought some fruit from an old lady who probably sewed uniforms for the Revolution. She carefully measured our purchases on a scale that was as old as she.

"Gee, Mike" TS#2 (who was a first-timer) said, "This is really quaint. I'm so glad you all asked me to come."

"Think nothing of it." My chest swelled.

TS#1 had been better places, so getting out of Charcas was more important.

"Where do we go from here?"

"I'm not sure."

Eyes rolled again.

"All I know is we don't want to go to Sta. Domingo or west. We must head for Moctezuma. That's south."

The reason Mr. Sanborn started writing the Travelog in 1948 was that things weren't always well-marked then. He'd have liked that area, since there was nary a sign to be seen. That didn't faze an old Mexico rat like me. I asked.

Mexicans don't give you wrong information on purpose. They just don't want to be impolite and tell you they don't know where you're going. Anyone will tell you how to get anywhere even if they've never even heard of the place you want. If you asked the way to Mars, it would be "two blocks, then left." What they mean is go two blocks and, God willing, you'll find some-body who knows where it is.

We toured Charcas several times then aimed west.

"Mr. **Mexico Mike**, aren't we supposed to be going south?" TS#1.

"You know how it is sometimes a road will go one way then an-other."

Never let 'em see you sweat.

The blacktop got potholes. We drove on the dirt. The dirt got

68

potholes. We zigged, then zagged. Sometimes an aged vegetable truck would lumber past us. They always left us a present of a cloud of choking dust.

The sun sank as we rolled into Sto. Domingo. Our dust cloud blew in behind us. When it cleared, we saw the airplane.

Not every little town in the middle of nowhere has a Cessna parked by the square. We thought it was pretty neat and Mr. Brilliant here wanted to take a picture of it. I was pretty tired.

Good thing for me, a guy who looked like he stepped out of *The Good, The Bad and the Ugly*, appeared from behind the plane. He asked where we wanted to go. I thought he was pretty nice to tell us how to get out of town.

Sunset on the plains of rural San Luis Potosi state is really magnificent. Since there are no towns anywhere nearby, there's no glare from streetlights. It's quiet, alone on the prairie, especially if nobody's speaking to you.

A pickup truck overtook us. Desperate for somebody to talk to, I motioned for it to stop.

"How far to Zacatecas?"

"*Lejos muy lejos,*" was the reply. (Man it's so far you don't even want to know).

The driver saw my face fall.

"But I know a shortcut," he said. "It's only three ranches to the highway."

Aha, I thought. How far could 3 ranches be?

We took his shortcut. A "*rancho*",

I now know, can be a long way away. When a person says they're from Rancho ——— , it means a settlement so small that it has to borrow a name from a nearby ranch.

I learned a lot on that trip, but it didn't get logged. I think it's better that way. I can't afford to lose any more friends.

"Mexico" Mike tries to stick to the main highway of life, but sometimes he goes off in a cloud of dust and has to learn the hard way.

69

Dan's Story: Brothers

Sunday, January 27, 1991

Dan Sanborn was my childhood hero. Still is. Thanks to him, I spent the best years of my life chasing a dream around Mexico while my ant-like friends were pursuing careers. Thanks to him, I finally caught the dream, right here in the Valley where I started out.

When Mr. Sanborn (he'll always be Mr. to me) told me he read my column, you'd think I'd been awarded the Pulitzer from the way my chest swelled. He even said it was ok — most of the time.

To help me out, he offered a couple of genuine Dan Sanborn anecdotes, told to him by genuine people. Now, I reckon these are the real McCoy, 'cause Venerable Dan wouldn't fib.

Not many folks stop in Tamazunchale (Tom as n **cha** lee) anymore. Like lots of U.S. towns, it fell into early retirement when the highway changed course. It's about 2 days south of McAllen on Hwy #85, which used to be the Pan-Am Highway. When the shortcut #101 was built from Cd. Victoria, tourism slowed to a few curious folks like me. I stopped there, about 15 years ago. I've got a car story about it, but that's for later.

There was one fellow, Dan disremembers his name, who stayed there in the '50's. He must have liked it, 'cause he died there.

A man's got a right to die where he damn well pleases, but few hotel owners are understanding, unless the deceased has paid in advance.

The owner of this here nameless hotel (it's gone to hotel heaven) was polite enough to try to find the stiffs next of kin. She found a name and address in Chicago.

"Hello, is this Mr. Dearly Departed's Brother (DDB)?", she must have asked.

"Yeah, what's it to you?"

"Is your brother DD?"

"So what?"

Somewhat taken aback, she continued. "Well, I'm calling from Mexico and he has expired."

"About time! That self-righteous so-&-so never did me any favors. Dump him in the closest river."

Now, Dan swears it went like this. Come to think of it, my brother would probably react the same way, if I had a brother.

"Ok, but what do you want me to do with his car?"

"What kinda car?"

"A brand-new Lincoln."

"Oh gee, I can't let poor old DD go to his heavenly reward alone. We were so close, you know. I'll be down as soon as I can. Just don't let the car get away."

DDB got to Tampzunchale within a week. The Lincoln was waiting for him. The hotelier, was pretty shrewd. She wouldn't give DDB the keys until he agreed to take DD back

70

That wasn't all. The grieving brother had to settle his late brother's bill. The hotel-keeper argued that he had occupied the room, even if he was a quiet guest, therefore he must pay.

The brother reasoned that he should pay half-price, since he didn't use the towels.

"No way José," the owner countered, "he used the sheets."

It wasn't the custom to embalm expired tourists, so DD

must have been on the verge of being ripe, so the loving brother didn't haggle. He settled the bill, dumped his blood-brother into the trunk of the Lincoln and roared north. I like happy endings, don't you?

$$$$$$$$$$$$$$$$$$$$$$$

I promised to tell you about a new hotel in Matehuala. It's called the **Parador Mision del Real** (PH: (488) 2-0641), and is on the

left, going south. Pass the old standby, the **Las Palmas** (PH: (488) 2-001). Just before you come to the welcome arch, turn left. There's a sign. There are 40 rooms and suites. The rate is $30 double (how else to travel?).

$$$$$$$$$$$$$$$$$$$$$$

"Mexico" Mike will probably grow up to be no good, if he ever grows up. Meanwhile, until he can find honest work, he continues to write Sanborn's Travelog.

Baja Goodbye

Sunday, February 3, 1991

Sometimes, to say goodbye, we have to go to Mexico. The land where death is a way of life is perfect for loosing the grip of the grave.

Cabo San Lucas, Baja California does feel like the end of the earth. For many, it is an end that enables a beginning.

My judgment, like anyone else's, is tinged by the past and what I expect in the future. In Cabo (even the locals call it that), I met a lady whose past was tied to the place and who had to return to free her future.

The Hotel Finisterra (Land's End), (PH: 3-0000 or 3-0100) has a lot going for it, though it's pricey ($150 & up for two). It does have a sauna, but no jacuzzi. Since it's full most of the time, unless you reserve months in advance, you won't get in. Also, sometimes the noise from the discos in town is disturbingly loud — but for some people, that's ok.

An excellent hotel which is less expensive ($60-80, double) and on the beach is the **Melia**. It has tubs in all the rooms, balconies and is quiet. The grounds are as tropical as you could want and the pool is sparkling, and heated.

At "Land's End" I met a lady I'll call Eleanor. Sure, I've got notes with her real name, but sometimes I feel like such a voyeur that I change the names to protect my sense of self-respect. People talk to me. They trust me, even after I tell them I'm a journalist. I don't know why, but they open up to me as if I were able to explain things about themselves to them. Hell, I don't even know what makes **me** tick.

Eleanor was standing at the bar by the Finisterra's icy pool. Yes, it gets pretty cold for a Valley boy in the Baja. Eleanor is 63, 5' 3", white haired, blue-eyed and beautiful in the ways that count.

I started a conversation with her, as I always do, asking her opinion of the hotel. Standard stuff. Resort conversation. It's light and easy and almost nobody objects to it. Usually, I take a few notes and move on to other guests.

Something about the way Eleanor hesitated when I asked if this was her first trip alerted my "story" antennae.

"No," she drew the word out for several seconds, "it's not really my first trip here, though I've never been here before."

"Ma'am," I drawled. I found folks trust you more when they think you're a hick. "Ah jest don't unnerstan' y'all."

"Maybe I'll tell you later."

I've learned enough about people to know when not to press them. I drifted away. You always see people again at a small hotel.

Sure enough, I saw her at the "Whale Watcher" about sunset. That's the "landmark" outdoor bar overlooking the ocean. Everyone at the hotel comes there. It's supposed to have the best view of the sunset in Cabo, but since the sun went down behind a small hill, I couldn't figure out why. In fact, I didn't see how it could ever set in front of the place, but local tradition (or advertising) says that's the place to be. Supposedly, you can see whales there, too, but I can't swear to that either.

Eleanor came over to me, since I was sitting alone (as I often do — roadloggers lead a very sad life). She pulled up a chair and we watched the whales that weren't and the sun that went in silence.

"What do you write about Mexico?" she asked.

"Oh, mostly the usual stuff: what the hotels are like, where to eat, what to see. Sometimes I get lucky and write something about the 'soul' of the country."

"Do you think you know the soul of Mexico?"

"I'm pretty egotistical, but not that much. I do feel that she grants me glimpses of it from time to time. That's what I share with my readers."

She considered for awhile, then looked straight at me with a gaze that went through my eyeballs all the way to my heart, my soul. I've only known cops who could do that before.

"You seem honest enough. I'll explain what I meant about this not being my first time here. My husband was a sailor. He sailed all the seven seas and I went with him many times. But we never got to Cabo together. He loved it so! He'd describe it with such fervor that I knew it was special to him. He made me feel the crashing of the surf against the "arcos", the blowing of the whales as they played just off the golden sand. He said we'd retire here."

"God had other ideas. He was lost at sea up in Alaska early this year. I spent most of the year in a deep depression, waiting for him to come through the door. It's awful when someone you love dies — it's even worse when you don't know if they're dead or just missing."

"Finally, I knew that he was gone. He came to me one night to say goodbye, he held my hand in the moonlight of my room back in Oregon, then vanished with the moonbeam he rode in on."

"I felt better, but still, I wasn't quite empty. There was one thing left to do. I came here, to spend some time with his memory, our last time together, before I commend him to the deep where he can rest."

Dusk had turned to night, but her eyes shone like beacons.

"So here I'll help him 'retire' from this earthly world, empty my heart of the longing to keep him with me, so that we can both be free."

She rose and moved to the railing. She stood staring out at the sea. The wind came up and blew her white hair and her white dress against the black night. It sang as the surf crashed and thudded against the rocks. I'm sure she didn't notice my leaving. I know when I'm the third wheel.

$$$$$$$$$$$$$$$$$$$$$$

Mexico Mike spends a lot of his time looking for people (or roads) that aren't there. When he realizes he's in McAllen, he goes to his office at Sanborn's and pretends to know what he's talking about.

Real de Catorce

Sunday, February 10, 1991

Real de Catorce is a ghost town. Even the 913 souls who live there are other-worldly. It's a mute testament to man's greed, and to his fickleness. I'm indebted to Lucy Wallace, a Valley writer who did much to promote Real, and authored a book, *The Incredible City*.

Nine hundred Mexicans and 13 lucky foreigners call it home. One of them is a beautiful Swedish painter, or so I'm told. I think my companions just made that up so I'd get out of the sack and drive around.

Once the 2nd richest city in the Americas, it was filled with 40,000 laughing, partying Spaniards and the wailing of the mestizos and Indians who tore the silver from the heart of the mountains surrounding it. The place dripped with luxury. There was an opera house, mansions, theaters, two coin mints, two cathedrals. Everything comes in twos here. The newer cathedral, built in 1780 is still in use. The floor is made of the tops of coffins. Unlike what some guidebooks say, there are no coffin bottoms with bodies underneath. We got to meet the bellringer, but more about that later.

Real was founded in 1773 by a black man, Ventura Ruiz, who stumbled across a rich vein of silver while looking for his lost mare. The story goes that he asked a local priest what to do with it, and of course, you know what the answer was. Actually, God and the King of Spain jointly owned everything in the Americas.

Everything about the place is shrouded in mystery and double meaning. It's name could be translated as "the Royal 14", which would tie in with the theory that it was named for 14 militia men hanged by local indians there. Or, it could be named for 14 bandits who used to hide out around there. Take your pick — always a good thing to do when going to a mining town.

To get there, take highway #57 out of Saltillo and flow southward towards San Luis Potosí. About the time you're ready to quit for the day, about 1.5 miles out of Matehuala, take a left to Cedral. Although you're only 32.5 miles from Real, it'll take you an hour to an hour and a half to get there. 13 (not superstitious are you?) miles are cobblestone and 1.25 are through the gut of the mountain via a one-way tunnel. For those of you who aren't familiar with cobblestone roads, make a comfort stop before you get going (or you'll have to on the way).

Bring a jacket, even in summer. It's 9,000 feet or 2,743 meters higher than the Gulf of Mexico. If you have trouble breathing, or are claustrophobic, think twice. The tunnel is pretty narrow in places. The traffic is regulated in a truly Mexican way. Sometimes there is a phone. No, there is always a phone: sometimes it doesn't work. When it does, the fellas on one end crank it up to tell the fellas on the other that the last car coming through is a cherry Mazda, or whatever. Then when they see a cherry Mazda emerge from this giant vaginal rock passage, they start sending cars the other way.

Now when the phones not working, the fellas hand the last car a red cloth flag wrapped around a stake. Probably does double duty as a vampire killer in a pinch. We were the last car through my last trip. I re-lived my high school track glory days as I clutched the baton, ready to speed it to the waiting man at the other end of the relay.

The tunnel is "open" (how do you "close" a tunnel?) 8 AM to 5 PM, though I suspect that neither is punctual. Other hours, you can still get through, but it'll be more fun. There are a couple of turnoff spots in it, right by the shrines to those who died there. Oh, did I mention the bats?

Once there, you'll be greeted by some aggressive, but friendly kids. I don't have many soft spots (except my belly) but even I'd help these guys. They're just trying to survive and offer a service at the same time. There aren't a lot of jobs in a ghost town.

The kids will try to steer you to one of the two hotels in town — **La Quinta Puesta del Sol**. I translate that as "the resting place for sunset." It's a little poetic, but by golly, it's true! The owner and his wife, Hector and Maricruz de Alonzo, are really great folks. The hotel is at the opposite edge of town on Calle Cementerio — you guessed it, cemetery street. It's just down

from, guess what? A cemetery, or rock garden, as my friend Mr. Ed calls 'em.

There are 20 spic-&-span rooms, with heat, shaped into a "U" around a little garden with a small Chinese pagoda. Beyond that is one of the most magnificent vistas of sheer powerful mountains I've ever seen. The mountains have rolled up there, covered with green trees, then split and undulated all around the hotel's property. When the sun sets there, it's like a picture window with a fireball. The only place I know that compares to it is in St. Lucia, in the Caribbean. There's magic there — power & serenity.

The hotel has a restaurant, which you should visit, even if only to watch the sunset. The kitchen is in full display on your right, in the old style. You can look right in and watch the cook peeling, then hear her chopping away and smell the soup simmering. Timid little girls will take your order.

At the end of the dining area is a roped off area, a monument to the son of the owner. You get the feeling you're in someones living room, a part of their lives. In fact, that's the feeling that makes staying at a small place so much nicer than a huge one, even if they have a jacuzzi. By the way, there are no jacuzzis in Real, unless one of the 13 foreigners had it.

The other hotel, the **Quinta Real**, is 1 1/2 blocks off the plaza. It's an old building, which gives it lots of character. Combined with the curving wrought iron staircases and decorative fireplaces, you couldn't ask for more character. I've stayed there, too, and it's a friendly spot. It attracts the European backpack type who can be entertaining. Sometimes, though, hot water is a bit scarce.

Rates for both are exactly the same — a mere $20-25 for two, right now, and more during the summer. Even then, they're less than $40. You can call and make a reservation for either hotel by dialing 011-52-4-2. That's the only phone in town.

§§§§§§§§§§§§§§§§§§§§§

Mexico Mike's "glory days" in high school centered around passing the jug instead of the baton, but we let him write Sanborn's Travelog when he doesn't suffer from "tunnel" vision.

Ghosts

Sunday, February 17, 1991

We all have ghosts. We all run from them now

and again. Some of us just run farther.

While in the ghost town of **Real de Catorce, S.L.P.**, I met a man who was coming home to face his ghosts. No matter how far we run, we never outrun ourselves. As Satchel Paige said, "Don't look back, something may be gaining on you."

He was a newspaperman; a Black man; a running man. He'd hid out in Mexico for the last 3 years, long enough for "people to ask if I ever really did work for a newspaper." He'd stayed long enough to heal. Mexico does that. She waits there patiently for those who need her.

I met Mark (not his real name — some people who report the news have a strange aversion to personal publicity), at the restaurant in the **Hotel Quinta Puesta del Sol** just before sundown. We talked through the deepening twilight. That's the real reason I like to travel — the people; the stories. That's what you'll really get from your trip if you're open. Mexicans, North Americans, Europeans, Asians, it doesn't matter. When we're on the road, we're all the same.

Mark had stories about Hunter Thompson, Norman Mailer and lots of others. What he didn't know was that he was more interesting than his stories of the famous and infamous.

What we don't realize is that most of us are the same

way. We all have our stories and they are all unique.

Mark was returning to Detroit to work for a big city paper there. He could have hung out in Cuernavaca and made a good living (heck, he got paid three times what I do for

a travel piece), but he wanted to make a difference. That's what he

said. What I knew was that he had to finish his atonement. That's the end of healing.

"Above all I'm a Black man. Maybe I can use what I know and what I do to help other Black men. Lord knows Detroit is a place that needs a lot of help."

I, like a lot of white guys, don't really understand — in my gut — what it means to be Black (or Chicano, or this or that). Oh, I do ok in my head, but there are some things, some feelings, that will always elude me. I couldn't admit that in the 60's — what liberal could? I'm older, have gone beyond liberal or conservative, and maybe got wiser. Life isn't black & white. It's all these shades of grey that just make everybody more alike. Today I can admit the things I don't know.

"I went deep into the Casa de Moneda, back in a dark corner. I could hear the screams of the slaves who dug the wealth that made this town so rich. It was founded by a Black man, you know."

78

"Yeah." Dan Sanborn may not have been Black, but he knew his history.

"I left the States," Mark continued after the waitress had lit a candle and brought his third 'Cuba Libre,' "because it was time for a change. The meanings of everything had changed on me. Nothing made sense any more. I couldn't see."

Sound familiar? Who hasn't been there?

He'd faded into the blackness just outside the elusive flickering light from the wobbly candle atop a tequila bottle. His disembodied voiced carried to me with the wind that wipped through the barrancas outside. Sitting on top of a 9,000 foot mountain in a city that had as many abandoned buildings as people, I knew he was the reason I'd been brought to that particular place.

"So I came to Mexico. I like it here. The people are warm, accepting. They know how to deal with stress. That's changing, sadly, but Mexicans are closer to the Source, to the magic of living than we are."

So, he bopped around, living the life of the Expatriate with a capital E, doing this and that until he was healed. When the time was right, he knew.

The same will happen to you, if you chose to let Mexico heal you. If you're at loose ends, troubled, go. You won't be alone. There are lots of broken people walking around the land of the Aztecs. Oh, they're not dangerously twisted, just a little bent.

There was "Cosmic Cowboy" in Palenque. Every night he sat at the same cafe table in a white 10 gallon hat, chaps, vest and bolo tie. He sang cowboy songs to himself. There was "A-16", a 60ish woman who returned to Acapulco, only she was stuck in 40 years ago. She played the same song over & over on the jukebox at a restaurant where her dead husband and she had been happy. She spoke not a lick of Spanish, but she was sure everyone understood her. When she made her peace with Death, she left.

There was, Josephina "the lady with the hat" in Pto. Escondido who created her own reality and was happy there. She gave me a typewriter as collateral for a small loan. I wrote my first unpublished book on it. She introduced me to literary agents who had never heard of her. One day she just went home, wherever that was.

There was "El Hombre Preparado" a 30ish, frightened gambler who couldn't figure out why everyone around him was dying or leaving; why his Midas touch had left. He had nothing left to lose, so he chose Mexico. He sat on cliff over the beach and wrote and wrote and wrote until his ghosts left to sleep in peace. He always carried a flashlight, & that's how he got his name. When the twilight of spirit left him and only the daylight of reality shone on him, he, too, packed up what little he had and headed North.

It's what we all do, when we have to. For us there will always be Mexico; for some of us there is only Mexico.

$$$$$$$$$$$$$$$$$$$$$$$$$

"Mexico Mike" is getting stir-crazy, being desk-bound, so we may tie him onto the back of a burro and send him somewhere soon. Until then, he's slogging away at updating Sanborn's Travelog.

Pto. Vallarta — Texans

Sunday, February 24, 1991

You just never know where you're going to find a Texan! Of course, you can always tell a Texan, but you can't tell him much.

You also never know when history is going to repeat itself.

Pto. Vallarta, Jalisco is one of my favorite spots. Once known as the "poor man's Riviera", it has grown into a popular "destination" as travel writers

and agents like to say.

Chances are, you've read about it before. The Vallarta I'm going to show you is different than the one other writers have shown you. It has a character that's unique. It's lusty, artsy and

a town of dreamers and schemers. I'll tell you where to stay and eat, but I'll also tell you about the characters who give it character.

In the old days (pre-1970's) DC-6 prop-jets lumbered over the mountains that separated "PV" from the world. By the way, back then "PV" was what the in-folks called it — today it's "Vallarta". Calling it "PV" today is like calling San Francisco "Frisco".

Then a road was built! That didn't "ruin" the place, as we know that folks who drive really appreciate and enjoy "real" Mexico. I don't care much for egotists who insist that everyone except them somehow "ruins" a place. Things change, and we have to change with them. True, I liked some places more when I was

one of the few gringos in town, but my friends who own the little restaurants & hotels are better able to feed their families now that there are more of us, so who am I to say it's wrong? I reckon that there were probably Mayans who got bent out of shape when so many barbarian Aztecs came and cluttered up their beaches and "ruined" the Yucatan. I don't think anybody was happy to see the Spaniards.

Still, if you don't want hordes of gringos to spoil your vacation, now's a pretty good time to do Vallarta. My friends there tell me that, thanks to the Iraqi-inspired fear of flying, tourism's down 60%-70%. Pedro Joaquín Coldwell admits to a 56% occupancy rate for Mexico overall, but cities with a lot of business traffic account for much of that.

I don't think there's been a single instance of a terrorist bombing a station wagon full of tourists. The BS you hear of "bandidos" on Mexican roadways is just that. Pack up the family (or girlfriends or boyfriends) and head on down to Vallarta.

Heck, Texans aren't generally known for being artsy types. Of course, we have just as many cultured folks as anywhere else, we just don't brag about it. We figure some things don't lend

themselves to being shown off —

81

unlike folks from less civilized states.

Gene & Barbara Peters aren't native Texans. They adopted us. Beaumont, TX was their home once. They love Vallarta for the same reason they loved Texas: "The people are so warm. We felt like we could be free around them." They own **Galeria Vallarta**, Juarez #263 PH: (322) 2-0290. They came to Vallarta when it was still called "PV". They liked it and stayed.

Gene's tall and fatherly. With his white goatee and soft voice, you're sure he's an artist, even though he says he isn't. I guess it's like saying you're not a writer if you don't write like Faulkner or Twain. Heck, we all just got to be what we got to be.

Barbara is small in stature, but not in spirit. She makes sure that things get done, that the doors open and stay open. She's managed to blend her Yankee "get-it-done" attitude with her adopted

Mexican "*en un ratito*" atmosphere.

Now they contribute to the community and to the art world. They spend time with customers and with young artists. Unlike some shop owners who are only there to push whatever they can on ignorant tourists, they actually try to educate them and give young artists a chance. Even if art isn't your bag, a visit to their shop will broaden your horizons, and maybe convince you to bring home something other than (another) tacky t-shirt.

Another Texan who calls Vallarta home is Rita Zanoni, who claims Bowie, Texas as one of her U.S.

homes. She's a well-known artist & sculptress/ceramicist who

often exhibits at the **Galería Rac, Lázaro Cárdenas #286.** She's full of life and a powerful personality. She didn't start out to be an artist. She held a lot of business-type positions before she settled into being herself. She found a spiritual side of herself that coexists with her management of the business of being a selling artist. It's a hard mix, one that few can achieve without tension.

That's the secret of Vallarta: it lets you be yourself, or find yourself. That's what many folks miss when they rush in and

out of the place. If you stay in your hotel compound, you'll only get to know your hotel. Get out, get downtown, a ways from the "Gold Zone" or Nuevo Vallarta and see what it's all about. Some folks find themselves here and some lose themselves. The choice is always ours.

Dick and Liz played here. See them play. One of my best friends in Monterrey tells me that he was here "many years ago" and got to dance with Elizabeth Taylor. We

were at the restaurant of the Ambassador in Monterrey. He's 70, with a twinkle in his eye that makes you suspect he's tuned into some cosmic joke that you'll never catch.

"I was a young man, it was before I married. I was walking down the street and I heard music. There was music everywhere in Pto. Vallarta. I looked up and there was this walkway between two houses. A beautiful lady was in one of them, dancing

"Oscar, weren't you scared that he would awaken?"

He smiled. "Of course! It was delightful. Imagine the tension of dancing with the most beautiful woman in the world in a strange town, while her husband snored in the corner!"

"We danced for an hour until the sun set. I watched it reflected in her eyes — red, red fire swallowed by blue sea, surrounded by a universe of green. I bowed, shook her hand and left. She spoke

little Spanish and then I spoke no English."

When he finished the story, he settled back into his chair and he gazed off into the distance, the past. Today he was just a distinguished old man, approaching Death. But for that one moment, he was a young prince, blessed by the siren queen of all time.

That's what Vallarta has to offer, memories unlike those you'll find anywhere else. There's a tension here, a sexual tension, an artistic tension, a creative tension. Leave your worry/work tensions here and tune yourself to a different frequency in Vallarta.

§§§§§§§§§§§§§ §§§§§§§

"Mexico" Mike says he danced with a beautiful woman once, but we all know he can't dance. He can't paint or play the harmonica, either. The only thing he does well is Sanborn's Travelog — & that's already written.

Pto. Vallarta

Sunday, March 3, 1991

There's more to Pto. Vallarta than art. Here are my favorite places to sleep around and fill my tummy. You can negotiate prices like never before! In fact, some hotels have closed entire floors due lack of business.

That's good news for the traveller. It's bad news for the folks who depend on us so they can earn money to pay the rent. The more I live, the more aware I am that everything is interconnected.

My favorite hotel is the **Molina de Agua** (Av. Vallarta, just over the bridge over the Río Cuale. PH: US — 800-826-9408, P.V. — (322) 2-1907). It's moderate ($30-40 US double) in price and rich in atmosphere, with one of the best jacuzzis in Mexico — a big stone tub in a rock grotto with a little waterfall behind it that's covered so you can get out of the sun and still get hot.

It has secure parking, 40 rooms, some bungalows and some suites — all different and all different prices. Enclosed by a wall, it's quiet, no matter where you pick. The setting is tropical, with parrots and a monkey who will snatch your glasses off your face if you get too close! There's a poolside restaurant where you can watch the monkey or the lassies, depending on your taste.

For luxury, the **Villas Quinta Real,** (Pelicanos #311, Marina Vallarta (PH: US — 800-445-4565, MEX (322) 800-36-015 —

cost: $110 US) gets my nod. It has 50 suites and 25 villas. The suites have jacuzzis and the villas have a private pool. The furniture is hand-painted from Michoacán. Classical music graces the lobby. The only member of the Small Luxury Hotels & Resorts, it's high on my list of experiences. Of course, you had to be there. Golf, tennis etc. are available.

When I need to save pesos, there are two main choices. Well-known by the college & backpacking set, the **Posada Roger** (B. Badillo #237, PH: (322) 2-0639, 2-0836 — COST: $14-20) is attractive with 52 rooms spread around a garden in 2 1/2 stories. The pool is on the second story! Some rooms, are a bit dreary, so check 'em out before you check in. The good ones are really nice.

Very nice for a budget-traveller is the **Encino** (1 blk south of Insurgentes Bridge, PH: COST: $11-18). It boasts phones, an elevator and rooftop pool and restaurants! But, you better like blue and coral decor!

If you've got a fantasy to live out, the **Garza Blanca** (White Heron), 4.5 miles south of town by Mismaloya, PH: (322) 2-1023 — COST. $150-200 US) is your best bet. I haven't actually lived out one there, but many celebrities have. It will pamper you. 57 units are set into a hilltop tropical setting. The villas have private pools, of course. There's a natural pool at a waterfall

84

nearby. For golfers, there's a 9-hole par-3 course.

The **Melia** (Marina Vallarta, PH: US: 800-888-5515 MEX: (322) 1-0200, COST: $120-150 US) is a Spanish chain and offers a health club, squash etc. It's always first-class in my book!

The **Fiesta Americana Condessa** (Av. Los Tules, off Airport Blvd, PH: COST. $90-120 US) has a health club with eucalyptus inhalation, herbal wraps, salt & mud treatments. A pastel gym tops the list! I've never rolled around in the mud, but *Eric the Heroic* says it'll make a new man of me — just when I'm trying to clean up my image!

The *Buganvillas Sheraton* (Carr. Aeropuerto #999, PH: US 800-325-3535, MEX: (322) 2-3000, 2-0513, COST: $90-110 US) has 12 stories, a wonderful view and two large pools.

There are three restaurants and one tamale stand that stand out. First is **Archie's Wok** (F. Rodriguez #130, PH: (322) 2-0411). Owners Archie & Cynthia Alpeula are nice, mellow folks. Archie used to cook for John Huston. Excellent Asian cuisine, white tablecloths, New Age music and reasonable prices ($12-18 for 2).

Pizza Joe's (B. Badillo #269, PH: (322) 2-2477) is owned by Joe & Claire — the sort of couple we all wish we could be. She runs the business and he runs the kitchen. They both do it well. The food's Italian (surprise!) and pizza. ($8-15 for 2).

Los Arbolitos (Camino de la Rivera #184 & the Río Cuale, (322) 2-4725) has good seafood and Mex-ican food. Overlooking river is pleasant. Very popular. ($8-15 for 2).

The best **tamales** in town are sold by a happily-wrinkled, brightly-aproned lady with a pushcart on the W. corner of the oneway N. bridge. She charges about a buck for one and Mikey couldn't eat more than 3. They're more like New Mexican tamales than the Northern Mexico or Tex-Mex varieties.

$$$$$$$$$$$$$$$$$$$$$$$$

"Mexico" Mike is so cheap he doesn't wear a watch so he'll have more free time. If he says something's a bargain, it's either free or stolen. You can find him squeaking in his office at Sanborn's Mexico Insurance.

Cd. Miguel Alemán, Tamps.

Sunday, March 10, 1991

I reckon I'm no different than most everybody else. I go gallivantin' off to far-away places when there's some pretty nice things right at home.

Cd. Miguel Alemán, Tamps. is a good neighbor of ours, just 54 3/4 miles west on Hwy 83, just across the Río Bravo from Roma, TX. I've been there as a guest of the *Canaco*, or Chamber of Commerce a couple of times, besides just poking around on my own. They're having a *Día de Comercio y el Turista* (Day of Commerce and the Tourist) next week.

Mark Sat. March 16, 1991 on your calendar. Starting at 9:30 a.m., the good people of the town will convert Av. Hidalgo into a pedestrian mall. After that, the good times will roll!

They'll have mariachis, cowboys, typical dancing, an artist's exhibition, bands like grupo Mantana & others & *Muchas sorpresas más* (many more surprises). Always a big hit, will be the crowning of the Queen of Winter Texans. They're going all out and we should all go out too.

Neighborly is a good way to describe Cd. Miguel Aleman. The folks who live there are very pleasant, hospitable, small town folks like you and me. They don't seem to be in as much of a rush as some places. They all seem to know each other and they genuinely like tourists.

'No hassle' could be their motto.

They're so honest, they even trust somebody as suspicious-looking as me. I stopped to buy some allergy pills from a *farmacia*. Since I get easily distracted, before I got to the drugstore part of the store, I had an armload of stuff. As the pharmacist patiently wrote it all down on a bill, I spied a notebook.

I picked it up and showed it to her. She nodded and kept writing. She was so sweet, she even smiled freely at one of my stupid jokes that don't make sense in English, Spanish or Swahili. That's courteous! She handed me the bill, which I was to take to the cashier. I dropped the notebook into the sack.

At the counter, I handed the cashier a $20 bill. She carefully calculated my purchase in pesos. The pharmacist signalled her. She counted the items in my sack, looked down at the slip of paper, then extracted the notebook. Oops! I realized what had happened. I hadn't been charged for it. The other stuff was drug items and the notebook was separate.

In some places, I would have gotten a dirty look. In others, they might have called the cops. Not in Miguel Alemán. With great ceremony and courtesy, the young lady took the time to explain what was happening, before she rang it up. I was embarrassed at being so stupid, but I've pretty much gotten used to that by now.

The folks there care about their community. They showed me a school where the students were well-behaved and genuinely proud of their school. Unlike many U.S. schools, there was no graffiti.

Feelings are one thing - action's another. In the computer class, the students and teachers stood especially tall. They had good reason. They'd gotten together, working, holding special events, to get enough money for a computer. They donated the machine to the school for future students. That's the future of Mexico — Mexicans helping themselves to the future, for the future.

§§§§§§§§§§§§§§§§§§§§§

We've been inundated with returning RV caravans. **Norm Yelland** (*Guatemala Norm*) said travel in Central America is easier than a few months ago. He

also said roads in Mexico are in great shape. He's leading a caravan to Panama, soon. **Bill Homlberg** of **Aztec RV Caravans** was particularly cheery. He'd found a mechanic in Oaxaca who could repair a Ford overdrive RV transmission. He warned the fellow to be careful.

"It's not a normal transmission," he said.

The Mexican shrugged, "So what is it — an overdrive?"

It just goes to show, never underestimate a Mexican mechanic.

Bill gave us a three-page list of gas stations on the Gulf coast and Yucatan that sell unleaded — Magna Sin. Folks, it's everywhere!

§§§§§§§§§§§§§§§§§§§§§

A really nice local fellow in a cowboy hat stopped by to chat. I really enjoyed his visit. He's one of those folks who spends a few

months down in Manzanillo. He told me about a new RV park there, Malamarimo, 500 meters from the glorietta. He called it *Chemo's*, 'cause he'd known the owner for years. That's what's nice about my job — I meet folks who make friends wherever they go. That's what travelling's all about.

§§§§§§§§§§§§§§§§§§§§§

Mexico Mike tried to pull the old 'I didn't know it was in the sack' routine back home. He got 30 days. He doesn't have any friends in any country, that's why he thanks those who help him to update Sanborn's Travelog.

Tripshare

Travelling alone is like a roller-coaster. Sometimes you're on top of the world and sometimes you're screaming on the way to the bottom.

Kids gravitate to me when I travel alone. I think it's because they can tell that I've been cast out by the pack and am easy pickin's for one of their devilish plots. By the way, I'm not a daddy.

I was once held prisoner in a sardine-can bus bounding from San Cristóbal de las Casas to Villahermosa by a 6 year-old whose only joy in life was tormenting motion-sick *gringos*. She was a cute one, all right. They all are. That's why I'm always in trouble. Cute chicks of any age are dangerous.

It was my own fault. I gave the mother a seat. She looked pretty tired. I reasoned that while I was tired, I was just visiting. For me, hard travelling was a lark. For her it was a fact of life.

Mama thanked me. She introduced her daughter. The child probably didn't meet many tall, blond, blue-eyed hunks. That's why she didn't mind settling for me. She pointed at the bus seat.

"*En inglés, ¿cómo se dice esto?*" she began in a cute sing-song.

"Seat," I began, aware of my position as an earnest ambassador of international relations. The mother looked at me gratefully. She was glad her little darling had this chance to learn English — or so I thought.

"*¿Cómo se dice,*" she paused and turned her disarming dark eyes at me (I've always been a sucker for dark eyes), "*esto?*"

Her sugar-coated fingers pointed to the book in my lap.

"Book," I replied, already tiring of the game. I opened it up and tried to read.

Soon there was a sugary fist tugging at my sleeve.

"*¿Cómo se dice,*" **point** went the fickle finger of my 6 year-old inquisitor, "esto?"

I may not be the brightest fellow in the world, but it dawned on me that this was going to be a **long** bus ride. I turned to the mother for help. She was snoring. I was in trouble. I knew from experience that any 6 year-old anywhere can outsmart me without trying.

To briefen it up, after 4 hours of this little game, as I swayed from east to west and sometimes north to south on one of the curviest roads in a very mountainous country, I understood why the mother was so grateful to me. It was probably the longest rest she'd had in the past six years. If I'd had a companion, he or she could have saved me, or spelled me. As it was, I had to pretend to be dead to escape.

Of course, I've been invited into peoples' homes because I was alone, and have met some folks who've become lifelong friends.

§§§§§§§§§§§§§§§§§§§

I've been getting a lot of calls from women who want to travel alone to Mexico. Of course, I always tell 'em they'd be better off going with me, but they seem to have better sense. Most of 'em mutter, "...when the well freezes over...", or something like that.

Seriously, it's a question that comes up a lot. You may not have known this, but lots of folks think I'm an expert on Mexico, so people call from all over. Well, it's not really (me) they think so special, it's Sanborn's. Venerable Dan must be proud.

Anyhow, several ladies (& a few guys) have asked me if it's safe to go alone. I've thought about it a lot, and give a different answer than I did three years ago — when I was an (unemployed) Mexico expert.

Most of your travel writers are women, at least the ones who do Mexico books. They generally bop about on their own. They encouraged me to let others know that, while there are some real drawbacks to solo travel, it's no different in Mexico than in Europe or the US. Rather than being worried about being molested, they were concerned about being helped to death.

A lone woman is going to get lots of offers of assistance from well-meaning males and solicitous concern from well-meaning women. A woman can allay most wolfish advances with a big hat and loose

clothing. Save the alluring stuff for when you're serious about alluring.

Many women team up after awhile, because it's easier to enjoy yourself with someone else there, or just because it's easier on the nerves.

There's a better way, though. We offer a free service called **Tripshare**. It's like an electronic college ride board. Send in some info about yourself, where & when you want to go & we'll enter you in our database. We mail a copy to everyone else on the list. Local folks can put a notice on our bulletin board at 2009 S. 10th. Before you get the wrong idea, not all are singles. There are many couples or RV'ers who want to share the experience with others. Write **Tripshare, P.O. Box 310, McAllen, TX 78502.**

An outfit that's far larger, and doesn't just do Mexico & Central America, is *Travel Companion Exchange , Box 833, Amityville, NY 11701*. They charge a fee, but give you a lot, like discount coupons and a very large database.

§§§§§§§§§§§§§§§§§§§

When Mexico Mike isn't scaring little kids, he's hardly working at Sanborn's Mexico Insurance, giving people misdirections.

Gas Jockeys

Sunday, March 23, 1991

March 18, 1991, was the 53rd anniversary of the expropriation of Mexican oilfields from foreign powers. Some gas-pump jockeys have carried on the tradition to this day. It was really a nice touch by Mexican President Salinas to close down the country's worst polluter — The 18th of March refinery in Azcapotzalco section of Mexico City. The man has class.

If I had to live in D.F. (as those in the know call Mexico City), like the Great Zamba, I'd be ecstatic. The place spit just about everything bad into the already thick air of the most polluted capital in the world.

Getting gassed (up) in Mexico has always been an adventure. I've looked on the gas jockeys as the last of a dying breed — highway robbers. Things have changed a lot, lately, what with the President himself leading the charge to honesty and integrity. In fact, you have to go out of your way to find a station that gives an old Mexico rat a real challenge anymore.

Most gas stations have really cleaned up their acts! Veteran travellers have been dazed by polite attendants, correct change, pumps turned back to zero, & even some clean restrooms! The government and Pemex have realized the value of the driving tourist and are making life easier for us. A fellow came in the other day and asked me when I was going to Matehuala next. Seems he accused the attendant of shortchanging him, and the poor kid made up the difference. Upon reflection, the tourist thought about it and by golly, he'd given the kid a smaller bill than he thought. He felt pretty bad, since the shortage probably came from the kid's pocket. He just wanted to get the change back to him.

If I hear too many stories like that, I'm going to stop listening. You can always tell a veteran Mexico traveller by the number of "Pemex" or "*gasolinera*" stories he has. Just to make sure the world hadn't changed too much, I sought out Juan Escarcega de Luis G., an old bandit from way back.

I found Juan in a *pulquería*, (about as far from a fern bar as you can get) tottering on the edge of a stool that tottered well enough without him.

"Juañ," I shouted over the "*ranchero*" music coming from the one-static-speaker jukebox in the corner. It took Juan a few minutes to respond to me. I think he was meditating in front of the neon-illuminated tapestry of the Last Supper over the bar.

"Ah," he whispered, "Miguelito! That'll be 150,000 pesos."

"No, Juan, you're not at work. You're in a *pulquería*."

He looked at me with his good eye — the bloodshot one. "Am I drunk?"

"Yes."

"Good! I deserve to be!"

90

"¿Por qué?"

"It's that new President! May the Devil take his soul! He makes it hard for a dishonest man to make a living."

"How's that?"

"It's all this honesty business. At first, like everyone else, I assumed he was just saying it — like all Presidentes do at first. I repeated 'todo es posible' with everyone else. Of course I went on with my business."

"That's cheating people who buy gas, right?"

"Sí; cómo no? (But of course!) How do you expect me to support my family and my pulquería on $4.00 a day?"

"Well, the theory is that if you provide good service, grateful people will give you a *propina* (a tip)."

Juan slammed down some pulque. "Get real." His eye brightened. The other was hopeless. "Remember when I got you by saying the counter on the pump was broken, so I calculated the price on my hand calculator?"

"Yeah, you got me for 66,500 pesos, and only put in half a tank. How'd you do that?"

"I taught the machine to add an extra 42% to the price. When I punched the numbers, you didn't realize I already had some in memory."

The man was a genius with a 3rd grade education.

"I almost stopped you with the locking gas cap," I countered. Let me explain. The most common way to overcharge is for the attendant to stick the nozzle into your tank as soon as you drive in. Like magic, you've paid 10,000 pesos too much. Don't think these guys wait for gringos to show up. They prey on locals, too. A peso is a peso.

"*Sí*, but I knew there would always be a way to distract you. When that happened, I cleared the pump as soon as you looked away. Of course, you remembered the true price, but I liked yelling with you. It was great sport."

That's the thing about the old stations. Overcharging was a game. Both sides knew that, but the attendants had all day to practice. Civilians never stood a chance. It wasn't a fun game, though.

A popular ruse was to count your change back to you very quickly, starting out at a high figure. Another is to "drop" your change, then make a great show of picking it up, palming some of it. When the guy hands it to you, all crumpled, you want to thank him.

Juan got me good once. I've always been slow with numbers, so I'm a pretty easy target. My bill was 54,000. I knew better than give my money a vacation by handing him two 50,000 notes, so I gave him a 50,000 and a 20,000. I was due 16,000. He brought out a handful of coins, apologizing. I noticed I was shy about 6,000. I pointed it out. He slapped his forehead in disbelief, then recounted.

"*Caramba*! you are right!" He was all innocence. He took back the coins and gave me more coins and a 2 brown bills. I assumed the 2 bills were 5,000. (Both the 2,000 & 5,000 note are brown and when dingy, look the same). I handed two of the coins to him as a tip for his honesty. I noticed an uncustomary twinkle in Juan's good eye as I started to pocket my money. Juan never twinkled unless he'd got somebody. I looked more closely, and sure enough, I had 2 2,000 brownies. I yelled at Juan to give me my 2,000 peso tip back. The boss came over, looked at Juan, me and shrugged. Juan gave me two coins. I was hot — always a mistake. He took the two 2's and replaced them with 5's. All seemed in order. As I walked away, he asked, innocently, "Where's my tip?" I told him where to go look for it.

Only later, when I went to pay for a Penafiel™ did I figure it out. The coins I had were not copper 1,000, but actually copper 100's. I'd been so intent on the paper money, I didn't pay attention to the coins.

$$$$$$$$$$$$$$$$$$$$

When "Mexico" Mike isn't hanging around Pemex stations, he's trying to figure out why people educated beyond the 2nd grade are smarter than he instead of working at Sanborn's Mexico Insurance.

Retirement

We're only on this earth for a short time. It doesn't matter **where** you live, it's **how** you live wherever you are.

I met one of the nicest couples this week. Bob & Pat Jacobs are the sort of folks who end up in Mexico because it suits them. They told me about Manzanillo — a place I'd discarded as not for me. So often we learn that what we thought was not for us was simply not for us at that time.

I reckon there are two types of folks who live in Mexico for the winter: those who just visit and those who get something from their time in the place they love besides some sun. You can always tell those folks — they're easy-going and truly believe that patience is a virtue. They're the kind of people I want to be when I grow up.

We talked about Mexico and things, sharing that instant rapport that Mexico afficionados have. They admitted that they just got tired of trying to explain to their friends here why they'd leave all this, Bob's arm expansively included the neat subdivision they lived in here in McAllen. I admitted that I sometimes got tired of explaining why I wanted to bounce around on the roads and play tag with dump trucks instead of have a real job. We simply did what we did because it was who we were. You can't explain that. You shouldn't have to.

"Imagine playing tennis in a place where the wind doesn't affect your game," Bob told me. "Imagine walking on the beach and not bumping into hordes of tourists. We'd tried Pto. Vallarta and found it was just too crowded."

That's one interesting aspect of growing older — we'd both been to the same place and had completely different views about it. That's what makes horse races and hideaways. Beauty and serenity are in the eye of the beholder. Neither of us was right, nor wrong. We simply were prisoners of our own perception.

The other type of winter Mexican may "live" there all year-long, but never truly **lives** in his adopted homeland. I see 'em all the time. They burst in and demand of me, "How many miles to Guadalajara?" or "What's the fastest route to Chapala?'"

When I start to explain to them that you don't measure distance in Mexico in miles, but in days of driving, they get impatient. They think I'm a young fool. That's okay, I'm just practicing until I can be an old fool.

I route them through the colonial cities like San Luis Potosí, Guanajuato, Lagos de Moreno and San Juan de los Lagos. I accidently ended up one time when I wanted out of Monterrey so badly that I asked for the next bus going South. I did the same thing in New York City's Penn Station and ended up in

93

Harrisburg, PA. I wonder if there's a connection I missed. Did I miss the bus?

About 1 in 10 will come back and thank me because they slowed down long enough to be entranced by the charm that is Mexico.

There are folks who live in Chapala and Guadalajara who are just wonderful and appreciate the country they live in. Some of them are very good friends of mine. I see my job as directing the first-time visitor who is on the edge towards learning how to enjoy Mexico and not just look at it as a place to escape the snow and sit around feeling superior.

A fellow came into my office who wanted to know about Manzanillo. A few days before, I'd have said it was an okay place and nothing more. Thanks to my new friends, I could tell him some of its advantages.

Don't worry, though. I won't sing the praises so loud the place will become lousy with gringos. After all, it's not for everybody. That's what makes it what it is.

To the fellow who came in, I gave the best advice I had. He wanted to arrange a place to rent in advance. I told him to drive down, stay in a hotel and see if he liked the place before he committed himself. Manzanillo might not be for him. Mexico might not be for him. I told him to buy an honest book about living in Mexico called (oddly enough), *Living in Mexico* by Michael Zamba. It's honest and good reading. Lots of retirement books aren't.

Easy does it. Take it a day at a time.

In Mexico, it's the only way to stay sane. Fortunately it's no guarantee that you will. Otherwise I would have quit going long ago.

A Gulf coast update: the **El Tajín** hotel in **Tuxpan, Ver.** has still not reopened. I was looking forward to rating the new jacuzzi the manager promised to put in. The management changed, so I won't hold my breath about the jacuzzi. I'll stop there in a couple of months and let you know.

Jeffrey Wilkerson, the authority on the ruins and author of the book, *El Tajín*, stopped by with his lovely wife. They dropped off some more of his readable books about the place. We'd sold out. That other media interviewed him! Ch. 4 will air it shortly. He's one archeology expert who's kept that gentle human touch that keeps him from being pedantic. Read, or watch, him.

When "Mexico" Mike isn't sending people off on wild burro chases, he's editing Sanborn's Travelog — the only guide to the highways of Mexico.

Capitalism

Sunday, April 7, 1991

I'm fixin' to go on the road again. That's the way we Texans talk for those of you not lucky enough to be one of us. I need to drive about Mexico to get stories for this column and to update Sanborn's Travelog. I also need to go because I just NEED to get back on the road. It's something I've given up trying to explain. I'm just grateful to powers greater than myself that I've got the kind of job that caters to my abnormalities, if not my immoralities.

Driving Mexico is my passion and my job. Many folks are afraid to drive. They have nothing against Mexico — they simply don't know any better. They're willing to fly in and enjoy a few days' relaxation on a sunny beach, or hop on a bus to a pyramid and say they've been to Mexico. They have and they haven't. It's like being only a "little" intimate. You miss the most gratifying part.

This trip I'll be driving a VW Vanagon. I've driven a lot of vehicles and each had a personality that made the trips special. When I drove my first ex-wife's powder-blue '65 Ford Mustang with the back seat removed, my trips were fast and utilitarian. In it, I learned about the soul of Mexico. I was on my way to being an import-export millionaire. I didn't. I did become the whip king of New Orleans, though. But that was long ago and in another country.

Julian was a young ambitious fellow who rented a stall in Monterrey's old market and invited me to his house to cement a trading arrangement. He wasn't a corporation and I wasn't either. We were just two young guys with big dreams and the freedom to pursue them. Our different nationalities were what made us need each other.

His house had a tin roof and thin plywood walls. Some of his neighbors had cardboard walls. Windows were squares cut out of the plywood, with a red-green-blue cloth remnant nailed over it. When the wind howled, it waved at us, blocking a little of the grey-ash cinders from the cooking fires and the steel smelter that operated there, then.

A red candle illuminated our meal of tacos and beans. His wife was young, shy, silent. She washed the blue plastic plates in a green bucket. Water came from two silver square cans that once held cooking oil. I didn't ask where the water came from. The tacos were good. The beef was stringy, the sauce full-bodied and chock-full of jalapenos. Little rivulets of grease flowed from the hot yellow corn tortillas to the plate when we raised them to our mouths. They were real tacos.

I drank beer then. So did he. He sent his oldest boy, a thin, dark, nervous lad of 6, off to get us a couple of *cervezas*. *"Bien fría,"* (good & cold) he hollered after the boy.

95

He proudly and gently showed off his children to me. His older daughter was 7, demure, who, like her mother, kept her eyes downcast. His baby was less than a year. She was quiet for a baby. The mother handed her to the proud papa, but never took her eyes from her. Mexican women are like all women — they know better than to trust men to be responsible.

The beers came, sweaty from having been in the *tienda's* (store's) ice-bucket. They were closer to "*al tiempo*" (room temperature) than "*bien fría*", but I knew enough to appreciate the effort more than the results. Maybe that's the secret to enjoying Mexico.

We drank and schemed by that one candle until we were lit and it wasn't. We shook hands on a deal that would start us both on the road to riches. Julian walked me through the "*colonia's*" maze of dirt streets to an unmarked corner where the bus stopped. He waited for it with me. Mexicans are good at waiting. I was learning then. We were both silent as we stood in the pitch dark so black we couldn't see each other. Disembodied voices drifted like fog around us, wraiths of humanity. Barking dogs grounded us in reality. He was probably thinking that his share of our profits would buy him a vehicle, a truck most likely, and a TV set and better clothes for his kids. Shoes would have been nice. I was thinking how odd it was; that I'd been given a glimpse into real life in real Mexico that I could never have seen if I hadn't been a capitalist pig. I was just beginning to understand that money isn't good or bad, but can be either or both.

The bus came, its pale, sickly yellow headlights hurting our eyes. It illuminated the rutted streets, the ramshackle houses and the road out of there. What it couldn't show was the dignity in my friend, Julian, and the warmth of the people in those houses. Some people ask me how I'm able to stand the poverty in Mexico. I see it, but I see beyond it. Mexicans are proud and may not be where we are materialisticly, but they are on the road. Give them a chance and they'll pass us.

$$SSSSSSSSSSSSSSSSSSSSS$$

When Mexico Mike isn't loaded, or trying to get on the bus, he's barely working on Sanborn's Travelog in McAllen, TX. It's the longest he's ever been employed.

96

Vehicles

Sunday, April 14, 1991

Folks always tell me what kind of car I NEED drive in Mexico. My 1965 Ford station wagon taught me that it doesn't matter.

"Get a Ford," they say. "You can get Ford parts anywhere."

Like most things that are true about Mexico, it's true sometimes. Whether your Ford's "hecho en México" or made in Detroit, you can get some of the parts all of the time, and all of the parts some of the time, but you can't get all of the parts all of the time — but so what?

Technology marches resolutely onward, but a simple Mexican mecánico with his pliers with black-taped handles, a green Phillips and a cracked orange flat screwdriver and a vise grip will outwit the technocrats in their white smocks forever.

The Ford met her first Mexican mechanic in Tamazunchale, S.L.P., on Hwy #85. We'd ventured off the road in search of "real" Mexico, thanks to a beautiful map that showed a "bosque nacional" (national forest) just off the hwy. Beautiful maps and women have always been my downfall.

We should have known we were in trouble when the road ended in a basketball court. Everybody politely gathered around the car, I guess to see if we wanted to shoot a few baskets.

"*Bosque*," I asked.

"*Sí*," the chorus of friendly folks repeated, "*el bosque*."

"*¿Dónde esta el bosque?*"

"*Más allá!*" they chimed. Twenty arms pointed in fourteen different directions.

We were surrounded by trees, so a trio of gringos asking where the forest was while standing in the town's basketball arena was a tad odd.

The road out of town, was politely called "improved" on our pretty map. As we climbed, it got worse. I insisted we go on. I was driving, so there!

The rocks got bigger and their resounding "ca-chunk's" against the bottom of the car got more frequent. The Ford shifted roughly. One companion was facing behind us (he was afraid to see the drop-offs before us).

"Mike, should we be leaving a trail?"

"Why so we can find our way back? Don't be silly." You just never know how silly people are going to be until you've travelled with 'em.

That's when the red and orange lights started flashing.

Even I'm smart enough to know when to quit. We parked, the Ford wheezed once and died. I found a busted transmission line.

"All we need is this simple aluminum pipe and we're set. There's a *"refraccionaría"* (auto-parts store) at the crossroads. I'll go back and get one."

"Whose damn fool idea was it to come on this road, anyway?"

"Sure, and they'll have a part for this old Ford just sitting there! You young fool."

Before my companions could turn really ugly, a logging truck lumbered by. With a hearty "high-ho aluminio" and an unmuffled roar, I was off!

In town, everybody wanted to help. "Sí," one was a mecánico. He was sure he could fix it. We went to his shop.

He didn't have the part, of course. No, they wouldn't have it at the *"refaccionaría"* either. He could make one, though. He rummaged around a his workshop and found some line about the right width. With a vise and vise-grips, he bent it to match the broken piece but a part was missing, a fitting where the line screwed into the transmission.

A trip to the auto parts store was mandatory. Of course, about a dozen of us went. The mecánico, sadly, had to stay, but he had great confidence that I, with my impeccable Spanish, would have *"un éxito"* (success).

Getting the threaded piece was easy. Getting the tool was hard. I knew I wanted an "easy-out", but no way I tried to translate it made sense. I made obscene gestures with my fingers and got a lot of laughs, so I quit. I was frustrated, having come so close, but kept so far from success. I just waved the busted fluid line and muttered *"roto"*.

One quiet middle-aged fellow, wearing a leather jacket and an air of authority stepped up and said, *"Vámonos."*

We went to his truck, — one of those jobs with drawers and boxes on both sides and lots of stuff in the middle. It was a serious repairman's trick. He opened a narrow drawer in the middle and gently pulled out a three inch metal instrument.

"Extractor," he said seriously.

There, in the palm of his calloused hand was the solution to my dilemma. With no knowledge of my language, he'd intuited what I needed and produced the solution. He refused payment. He worked for the highway department and the tool was not his. He would "loan" it to me. I was to return it to the store the next day. Without listening to my gushing thanks, he stepped up into the cab of his white steed and sped off, soon lost in the distance and the setting sun. In Mexico, there is always a way.

§§§§§§§§§§§§§§§§§§§§§§§

When "Mexico" Mike isn't busting something, he's ramrodding Sanborn's Travelog into shape.

Pan American Highway

Sunday, April 21, 1991

Nobody has ever accused me of being easy to get along with, or called me neighborly. Still, neighbors are a pretty nice thing to have. I guess mine are so nice to me because we allow writers (and other crazy people) a wee bit of latitude.

Gene Buckman putted up to my house on his motorbike a few weeks ago to find out if I was the guy who made up all that stuff about Mexico. I admitted it and we talked about our likes and dislikes. The other day he putted up again with a book, *down that Pan American Highway*, by Roger Stephens.

Mr. Stephens explains why many folks don't venture down the road, "... the fear that it will cost them too much and the fear that 'sumthin' orful's going to happen' ...." I reckon things haven't changed much since 1948. He says "In a single year, more than 100,000 pleasure vehicles rolled comfortably over the 763 mile all-weather, well-paved stretch from our Texas frontier to Mexico City."

Written in 1948, it chronicles one of my favorite roads, Hwy #85. In 1924, the automobile industry was worried about having reached a saturation point and was looking for new markets. Mr. Stephens tells us that the auto industry, in conjunction with heavy equipment and supply manufacturers, financed a project to bring representatives from nineteen Latin American countries to study our road system and construction. Mexico began construction in 1926, from Nuevo Laredo to Mexico City.

One of his first chapters is "Is it Dangerous?" He asks "Is it really safe to venture even as far south as Mexico ...." He recounts a litany of muggings, chases by coke-heads, being swindled and murders. Of course, all these happened in Manhattan, not Mexico. "All manner of crimes, petty, and great are committed daily all over the world. Yet in travelling ... for these thirty-odd years ... no untoward incident occurred ... other than one or two scrapes for which my tactlessness alone could be blamed."

He had a good idea of the heart of Latin America, "Color appeal, sound appeal, & heart appeal are always close at hand. Even the most hard-bitten banker will find a refreshing contrast. Here the heart and soul of one's fellow man are the true measure of character rather than the [his] assets."

Maybe he's a little naive, and I know one or two bankers who know the true measure of a man; whose hearts are as big as Texas, but his sentiment is laudable.

The book's full of the ways thing's have changed and the ways they haven't. Roger (you'll feel like you know him personally when you read the book, to) stops in Laredo, Texas for, "... the last prerogative of the

American taxpayer (filling my fountain pen at the Post Office)." At the time it cost more to cross from North to South. Today the differential's still there, only it goes the opposite direction.

Roger feels that, "Dear old Tamazunchale, (SLP) is a mess, thanks to American travel. I am shocked to read over one hotel: 'WELCOME TOURISTS, AIR-CONDITIONED, MAXWELL HOUSE COFFEE, AMERICAN FOOD, CURB SERVICE.' Another offered: 'Habitaciones con Equipo Simmons (rooms with Simmons beds).'" He was surprised to hear a street band blare the 'Beer Barrel Polka!'

An interesting item is that the police in Mexico City who were proficient in languages other than Spanish drew extra pay and proudly bore on their sleeves flags of the nations whose language they spoke. "As a neat backhanded compliment to the Colossus of the North, not once did they display the Stars and Stripes, but in its place the Union Jack of England."

You'll like Roger for his observations about the kind of traveller nobody admits to being. "Confining their trips to super-duper places ... they scurry only to flashy Americanized hotels to ferret out the swankiest Americanized bars, night clubs and half-breed honkeytonks (my favorite kind!). Fraternizing only with those who speak American ... they speak disparagingly of the very folks whose hospitality they so avidly accept." Why do they subject themselves to travel? "Maybe it's just sloughing off inhibitions away from Main Street, down where personal identities are unknown and where tales are less likely to be told."

"Teachers, ministers, artists, writers, secretaries or what have you (any and all who are sympathetically imaginative) ... I am happy to report my own experiences in Middle America. One thing I promise those courageous enough to make the plunge is a rare combination of much that is beautiful in nature with that which makes the whole paradise setting must so much more enjoyable — universal generosity and a cordial welcome from our Good Neighbors in all seven countries through which their paths may lead." Amen, Brother Roger, amen.

$$$$$$$$$$$$$$$$$$$$$$$$

When Mexico Mike isn't being a bad neighbor, he's on the road. That's where he is right now, checking out the West Coast for Sanborn's Travelog. His neighbors are having a party.

Dan's Story: Stuffed Grandmother

Sunday, April 15, 1991

I just can't go very long without a genuine Dan Sanborn story. For those few who don't know him, he's the "Father of Automobile Tourism." I kind of adopted him a long time ago and he's so good-natured that he didn't object to this sullying of his family name. One of his favorite stories is about the stuffed grandmother. He began selling Mexican auto insurance from Mc-Allen, Texas in 1948, along with orange juice and horny toads. For those of you who aren't from these parts, they aren't amphibians with inadequate love lives. They're lizards that shoot blood from their eyes when they get really upset.

Venerable Dan used to drive the Mexican highways and jot down notes about where to turn left or right and where neat little "out-of-the-way" spots were. He gave them away until somebody suggested he use them to encourage folks to buy his insurance. He did and the tradition continues today.

Although you may recognize a similar incident in a Chevy Chase movie, this is the "original" version.

There was this family, Big Bubba, son Little Bubba, mother, Becka, daughter Bonnie and grandma Prudence who took off from Baton Rouge, La. to explore old Mexico in the 1954.

Barely into their trip, Grandma chose to make her transition from this life to the next in Tampico,

Tamp. I reckon if you've got to make a transition, Tampico's as good a place as any.

Well, Big Bubba was frugal. He didn't want to waste time and money going home — he still had a week and a half vacation left. The family decided they had to find a way to go on a'goin'. Gramma would have wanted it that way. The only hitch was that embalming wasn't and still isn't a common practice in Mexico. It was summer. Grams would ripen pretty quickly.

Big Bubba reasoned that since Tampico was a sport-fishing town, and many folks kept mounted memories, that a taxidermist might fill the bill. The hotel manager knew one. How they got Grandma down the stairs and into the car was never explained.

The *taxidermista* immediately understood the problem (it was August). He said he could do it. Stuffing is stuffing. He took a tape measure and measured Grandma from fin to beak — I mean toe to head.

"*Señor*, your *abuela* (grandmother) has the same meters as a medium sailfish. Therefore, I will charge you the same price as for that fish."

That seemed reasonable, but Big Bubba negotiated, since he didn't want her mounted on a plaque, or have a brass plate with her weight and date of catch. The *taxidermista*

101

gave the dear old lady a toothsome smile, and molded her into a sitting position, so it would look like she was a happy passenger.

The family returned the next day. Everybody thought she looked happy and lifelike. Hands were shook all around. The *taxidermista* and grandma both wore proud smiles.

The family put Grandma in the back seat with a shawl over her lap, and rolled south. *Tuxpan, Ver.* so reminded them of Baton Rouge that they all got a little weepy. Little Bubba said Grandma's cheeks were wet, too. In *Veracruz,* the place felt so alive and like their beloved New Orleans, that even Grandma started to La Bamba!

On the way home, they detoured to *Jalapa, Ver.* for some cooler air. One night their car was missing — along with Grandma! They reported it to the police, who were very solicitous and hopped right to it. The next day the car was found!

"I am very embarrassed, *señores*," the police inspector told them with downcast eyes, "but your possessions were taken from the automobile. If you will make a list of the missing items, we will leave no stone unturned until we find them."

Now these nice folks from Louisiana looked at each other and back at the inspector and didn't know what to do. They were a little fuzzy about Mexican law regarding corpses, but suspected that mentioning their stuffed grandmother at that point would only complicate matters. They didn't. Big Bubba dutifully filled out an official form in tripli-cate listing the missing items, except for one.

They returned home happy with their experiences in Mexico. Their insurance company was happy that it didn't have to pay a claim. Grandma was happy at all the extra touring she got to do. The only unhappy person in this tale is the thief, who couldn't figure out why some crazy gringos would stuff an old lady like a big fish, then leave her in the car. Not only that, but he's sure he could make a lot of money selling her, but how?

Mr. Sanborn assures me it happened just like that. How could a young whippersnapper like me presume to doubt it?

$$SSSSSSSSSSSSSSSSSSSS$$

We think Mexico Mike has lost his marbles and can't tell the difference from an old lady and a fish. Now you know why he's not a sportswriter.

How to Stay Out of Hot Water

Sunday, May 5, 1991

Mexico's very much like the rest of the world — and a lot different. I feel at home there, not because I'm fluent in Spanish or an expert on Mexican culture, but because I've never felt at home here.

Maybe it's because I don't think logically; don't expect things to work out in an orderly fashion; am constantly surprised by the mundane. I mean, if you're the kind of person who literally forgets which tap turns on the hot water — in your own house — then you'll probably feel at home in Mexico, too.

Got to talking to a friend and reader the other day. (Some wiseacre said he didn't think I had any. He jumped out of the way before I could ask which one he meant.) "Mike," he said, "I think your stories are really interesting, but how about some help for those of us who don't know our way around like you do?"

If you're willing to take advice from a guy who only discovered that the sofa in his three-room trailer was a sleeper after three months, read on.

It seems this fellow went to the charming little city of Zacatecas (which everyone should do, by the way) and while he and his wife had a delightful time, a few of the oddities of Mexico puzzled them.

Q: Why is it that the elevators had a button labeled "PB"?

A: Some say it's to bamboozle tourists and other unsophisticated folks from the outback, but a more frequent answer is that it stands for "planta baja". Either way, it means the ground floor. Punch "1" and you'll get out on the second story. No foolin'. I asked a linguistic authority about the meaning of "planta baja" and she said it meant ground floor, or possibly low-flying plants. So when a Mexican tells you that a building has 12 floors, it probably has 13, unless, of course, he doesn't subscribe to the "PB, 1st floor (really 2nd)", theory. Really. Some elevators have "lobby" for the lobby and "2" for the second floor. Some have lobby and "1". Your best bet is to count 'em yourself. Or, unless you're an engineer, don't worry about it.

Q: Why did my wife get scalded when she turned the tap marked "C"?

A: "C" stands for "caliente", which is "what a chili pepper is". "F" means "frío", which is what the poor man's wife wanted to be. I've found that women often have different definitions of hot and cold than men. Don't be fooled into thinking this one is standardized, either. You'll see plenty of faucets with an "H" on them. The other may be "F" or "C" or something in Japanese. Some fixtures were imported from the U.S. or somewhere else equally bizarre.

Unfortunately, this befuddled the Mexican plumbers, who said "the heck with it" and began slapping on handles willy-nilly. Not content

103

with confusing soapy Mexican and gringo bathers alike, some foul fiends actually reversed the water pipes so that the hot can be on the left or the right.

Q: I thought there wasn't enough hot water in Mexico?

A: Not true. You can burn your bunions at most every hotel that is a class above budget that you want. I've certainly been in enough hot water wherever I've gone.

Q: Why is everything *"dos cuadras"* (two blocks) away?

A: My theory is that this is a self-protectionist measure learned by the Indians of Mexico to get rid of the Spaniards. Whenever they'd ask where the gold was, they'd torture any poor Indian who told 'em he didn't know. If, however, he said it was "just over the next hill", they'd leave him alone and gallop off in greed.

Actually, it's more complicated. To tell someone that you don't know where something is can be considered impolite, and damaging to the ego of the person asking. It can also give the impression that you aren't very smart, which is damaging to your ego. Either way, you have to say something. Just think of it as meaning that, 1) Either the place you seek really is only two blocks away, or 2) Man, I don't have the foggiest notion, but I'm sure that if you go about two blocks away and ask someone else, they'll know for sure.

What I do is ask three people. If two answers agree, I go that way. Of course, that's not fool-proof either.

We've only scratched the surface of the oddities that make traveling in Mexico an experience, if you keep your eyes and ears open and are willing to go with the flow — even when the flow is out of the "wrong" tap. Try to remember there are no rights or wrongs, only differences. You'll get along a whole bunch better.

§§§§§§§§§§§§§§§§§§§§§§§

"Mexico" Mike probably looked pretty silly, hopping around on one foot, all lathered up with no place to go. We keep sending him off on wild faucet chases for Sanborn's Travelog, but he keeps finding his way back home. Next time we won't let him take any bread crumbs.

104

Itinerary — Border, Cd. Victoria, Gulf Coast

Sunday, May 12, 1991

Folks, I thought I'd give you a few driving trips to take your mind off whatever it's been on. These are some trips you can take in a few days or a few weeks.

Many of Mexico's most interesting attractions are within a day or two's drive of her borders. **Cd. Victoria** is a mere 4 hours south of **Brownsville, McAllen, Laredo, Texas,** yet offers true small-town hospitality, black-clad Mennonites selling their crafts, a natural grotto where the Virgin Mary appeared and a miracle happened to Mexico Mike, a natural waterfall and one of the best bass fishing lakes in Mexico.

Due south of Cd. Victoria, a mere 3 hours more is **Cd. Valles,** where you can spend the night at the **Posada Don Antonio** and visit nearby **Xilitla,** where an eccentric Englishman, Edward James, built a castle and a sculpture sanctuary in the middle of an orchid jungle. He was a pal of Salvador Dali and Picasso. His works are surrealistic and amazing, set in the tropical setting. The fellow was quite odd. He had an idea that deer could live on the native diet of corn and tortillas & beans. They couldn't, but it was an interesting idea, anyway.

A little to the east of Cd. Valles are sulfur springs, at **Tamuín,** reputed to cure what ails you. There's a nice hotel there, the **Tanninul** which doesn't have a TV and is quiet.

If you're a water-baby, the **Gulf Coast** is readily accessible. Within 5 hours on Hwy #180, is **La Pesca,** which offers great salt & freshwater fishing, hunting, unspoiled (for now) beaches, and laid-back small-town atmosphere. This month's copy of *Texas Monthly* will have a story about La Pesca by Joe Nick Patoski. He and I rolled down there a few weeks ago and we both liked it. Three hours south is **Tampico,** a bustling seaport with an international atmosphere.

The ruins of **El Tajín,** an archeological zone of 2640 acres, are but another 3 hours south, near **Poza Rica, Ver.** According to noted archeologist, Dr. Jeffrey K. Wilkerson, in his book, *El Tajín,* "El Tajín is one of the most important archeological sites in the Americas. This ancient city has attracted visitors for two centuries. It's significance lies not only in its considerable size but in its many unique attributes which include very distinctive styles of art & archeology."

It flourished during the Classic Period (circa 300-900 AD) and was a city of the Totonac peoples.

Just a tad south is **Papantla,** noted for vanilla and brujos or witches. If you like your witches in plain vanilla, I reckon this is the place for you to go. There's an okey-dokey hotel on the square. Don't go out after dark alone.

Half a day's drive farther south

brings the visitor to **Veracruz, Ver.**
— one of the most *alegre* cities in
the hemisphere. Like New Orleans,
Havana and San Francisco, CA, it's
unique, with an atmosphere all its
own. Eating and history are just two
of the interesting things about the
place. Every character who invaded
Mexico or was forced to scurry
home came or went through here.

A few hours more and you're in
Catemaco, site of a mysterious vol-
canic lake and land of witches. From
here, another few hours takes you to
excellent tarpon fishing and
birdwatching. The next day you
could be in the jungles of **Palenque**
and the forests of **Chiapas.**

You're not limited to this, and can
drive all the way to Chiapas, to **San
Cristóbal de las Casas** where shy
Indians in colorful everyday garb
make you aware that you're near the
Guatemalan border. I like the place
because it has a funky steambath,
sauna deal. Of course I'm interested
in history and culture, too.

You can drive to **Cancún** and re-
ally **see** the country and not just the
first-class accommodations it offers.

*Mexico Mike doesn't spell too well,
so we're not sure what kind of
witches he's talking about.*

Mountain Kingdom

Sunday, May 9, 1991

Gosh, folks, some people have accused me of having water in the brain the way I talk about the Gulf coast and such. Ok, I promise you can drive south (and west) and not get your feet wet. I won't even talk about a jacuzzi this week! This week, we'll drive through what I call the mountain kingdom. Actually, we'll only do part of it, cause it's so big.

If the coast doesn't interest you, take to the mountains! Three and a half hours out of McAllen, you'll be in the third largest city in Mexico, **Monterrey, N.L.** For over a million visitors a year, this is their first taste of "real" Mexico.

Going south on Hwy #85, you can drive through lush farming country, pass citrus orchards, get fresh-squeezed juice from roadside vendors. The money you spend here will go directly into the economy. Some of my best memories are of dealing with these local folks. They are kind, gracious and have good deals. Many folks are afraid of venturing away from the "mega-resorts" because they don't speak Spanish. Well, I'll tell a little story on myself.

When I first started driving here, it was 1968 and I was a mere child. I flunked Spanish in high school. I learned a few words and read in Dan's *Travelog* that a smile was worth 100 hours of practice or something, so I smiled a lot. I knew that many times just adding an "a" or "o" to English words made Spanish words, so at hotels, I asked for "*sopa por el baño*." If you don't know, that means "soup for the bathroom." The Mexicans are so gracious that none of them laughed and nobody filled my bathtub with soup!

Cutting west a little farther, you can go through the magnificent Sierra Madres and pass the wonderful mural **"Los Altares"**, depicting Mother Nature holding an ear of corn, Mexico's staff of life, an oil derrick and other representations of the strengths of Mexico. It was cut into the black rock side of the mountain by sculptor **Federico Cantú**, back in Sept, 1961. It was here that Presidente López Mateos dedicated the highway. Not the altar underneath the sculpture. Each of the lighted candles was placed by a traveller on the road. It's said that truckers light one coming and going in thanks for making it on one more run.

By nightfall, you can be in **Aramberri,** a little "typical" town that boast one hotel, some ancient trees and a waterfall. Quite a change of pace. Farther west is **Real de Catorce, S.L.P.,** once the second richest city in the world! Today it's a ghost town with lots of history and an entrance though a tunnel in the middle of the mountains. There are two tourist hotels and lots of breath-taking views.

From Monterrey going west is

Saltillo. It's a mile-high and only 40 miles on a four-lane expressway. It was once the capital of Texas and many Texans had summer homes there. I've heard that Stephen F. Austin and Travis and all those guys had places here. Could any of you who know write me care of this newspaper and let me know if it's true? Thanks.

No road trip would be complete without a visit to ZACATECAS. It's an old, old mining town (founded in 1546) and is one of the most interesting in Mexico. You'll find no better example of "colonial Mexico" than this. Its original name was *"Most Noble and Loyal City of Our Lady of the Zacatecas,"* which was bestowed on it by King Don Felipe II. It was also known as the "King's Mines." It's an intellectual city, with a university and has a Spanish colonial flavor. Literary discussions take place in several coffee-shops scattered about. The city's motto is "Zacatecas es puro corazón" (pure or all heart).

The 300 year-old cathedral is quite interesting, especially its very ornate facade and art work. Baroque is the style here. There's a cable car *"telférico"* that goes up to the summit of Cerro de la Bufa from **Motel Del Bosque** (or you can drive if you wish over a paved road). where there 's a pretty church and big plaza. There are also shops that will sell you just mementos, especially those made of stone. The view of the city is absolutely spectacular, especially at night. Another interesting thing to do is to enter an old mine, the *"Mina El Edén"*. It's chilly, so bring a jacket. Bear in mind that their "La Feria" (fair) is held annually on September 1-15, so be sure to make advance reservations if you plan to visit then. There are many shops in an underground mall thing downtown, called the **Mercado Principal**. One sells a very large variety of leather coats.

Itinerary — Nogales — Mazatlán — Durango

Sunday, May 26, 1991

I ran into an old high school chum the other day. She asked if I was the guy who wrote those columns in the paper. I looked around for someone else to blame it on, but it was too late. I 'fessed up.

She said, "I thought so. It sounded like you."

Well, I reckon that a rotten apple doesn't fall too far from the orange tree or something like that. Funny, though, I thought I'd gotten a whole bunch different than when I was 16, but I guess not. So if there are any young aspiring writers out there (who read my drivel), don't count on getting much different, just try to get a little better. Heck, that's pretty good advice for all of us.

Just to let you know that I'm not stuck on the east coast, I'm going to take you over to the Pacific side of Mexico. You can get there from here or from Arizona. Let's just pretend that you went to visit that foreign country of California and wanted to come home the scenic way. Follow the freeway like a lemming and take a left in Tucson.

From Nogales, AZ, you can drive to San Carlos in about five hours via 4-lane highway. It's a nice beach town with palm trees and a majestic rocky coast. You've probably already seen it. The movie *Catch 22* was shot here. It's got a lot of gringos living there and Club Med has established a beachhead, but the stark scenery of desert juxtaposed against ocean make it pretty interesting for those of us whose first idea of what an ocean is supposed to be came from the Gulf of Mexico and Padre Island.

Keep going south and you'll *ruin* into Álamos — a place that's trendy and ghosty at the same time. It was about to be destroyed when the Rockefellers, DuPonts and other folks richer than I got together and helped it become a national shrine. It reminds me of Santa Fe, NM, or Bisbee AZ.

You could go a few more hours and catch the famous "Copper Canyon" train in Los Mochis. Leave your car at a hotel and enjoy one of the most spectacular rides in the continent! You can't fly and do this!

Within another day, you could roll into Mazatlán, sport-fishing capital (or one of them) of Mexico. Along the way you'll pass good bass fishing. You regular readers will remember that I once caught a fish here. Okay, I'm not Hemingway and it was a sailfish, not a marlin and my hands didn't get bloody, but I felt pretty macho, let me tell you. It was a true fish.

Turn east to Durango and you'll pass Concordia, a small town known for furniture-making. In fact, they have a huge statue of a rocking chair in the town square! A few miles beyond is an "artsy" settlement, Copala, Sin. A little farther up the road, you can eat sauerkraut in a German restaurant/hotel in the alpine-like mountains, the **Villa Blanca**. By the end of the day you can sleep in an old convent in **Durango**, site of many Western movies and *Fat Man, Little Boy*. I slept in the same hotel as the Hollywood crowd and got a casting call for the next days shooting! Maybe you will too!

And, of course, if you need a mechanic, there's a heck of a good one here!

Ice

Life's simpler and easier when you're well. Even ol' Mike finds it harder to cope when he's injured. Of course, that's when I find out what I'm made of. Reckon that's why the good Lord gives me so many chances to hurt myself — He's just trying to let me figure out who I am. Sometimes I do wish He'd give me a hint without knockin' me on the noggin so often. 'Course there are those who say it's my least damage-able spot.

I'd like to say that I injured my foot while saving a boatload of people from drowning off the coast of Isla Mujeres. I did say that for awhile. Folks believed me too. Then I tell the truth — I turned it on a loose rock on a path.

A simple twist of Fate. No big deal. I'm Texas-tough, Valley proud. I didn't need a doctor. Ice. That was the ticket. Put enough ice on my swollen ankle and I'd be fit as a fiddle. Things have changed in Mexico. The last time I needed ice, I called the bellman, he brought some up and I tipped him. Simple. Now it's not.

I've never been a fan of "*servibars*." For those of you fortu-nate enough not to know, they are little refrigerators that infest first-class hotel rooms in Mexico. They're chock-full of stuff to tempt you, like itty-bitty bottles of booze (that cost more than a real bottle), *Cokes*™, peanuts, candy bars and cigarettes. They cost a small fortune and always complicate checking out. Even when you don't have 'em opened, the front desk has to send someone to check it. I've learned to drink an "*agua mineral*" (mineral water) a day from them since I'll be charged for it anyway.

The servibar makes ice in cute little trays that are fine if you're having a dainty drink, but useless if you've got an ankle the size of Godzilla's — and the temperament to match.

"This is room 2,136,789. (I was in Cancún, home of the mega-hotel.) Please send up a "*hielera*" (ice bucket - a valuable word learned after years of fumbling.)"

"Señor — isn't your servibar open?"

"Yes, but I want lots of ice."

"Very well sir. I'll send a bell-man."

Sure enough, after about 20 min-utes, a guy showed up with an ice bucket. Of course there was no ice in it. He opened the servibar. I thanked him and asked for some ice. He'd be pleased to get me some, but I would have to request it from room service and he was a "*botones*" (bellman).

I stumbled over the to phone, my ankle and my mood getting blacker by the second.

"I just want some ice."

"I'm very sorry señor, but we can-

111

not send ice by itself. We can send you a bucket of champagne in ice. Would that be acceptable?"

"Why would I want champagne — to celebrate getting some lousy ice?" Even Mexico Mike isn't always pleasant and understanding.

"I'm sorry sir, I do not understand."

"It's a good thing for both of us." I called the public relations. After all, I have clout!

"How may I help you Mr. Mexico?"

"Look, I have to apologize if I'm abrupt, but I've injured my ankle and am in pain."

"That's terrible. I'll send up a doctor right away."

"No!" I shouted. "It's just a sprain. All I want is some ice."

"No doctor?" He sounded hurt that I'd refused his *médico*. "Our doctor speaks English and studied at the University of Texas."

"Thank you, really. It's just a sprain. I'm sure he's great. All I want is some ice."

"Then why are you calling public relations? I will transfer you to room service."

"No, wait ...."

"Room service."

"Hook 'em Horns." I hung up.

I whimpered for a little while, staring out at the crystal-clear Caribbean waters and thought about all the folks who envied me and where I was. Never judge somebody's inside by his outside. I vowed to be more tolerant and understanding of people who complained about the frustrations of travelling. I'd have taken a vow of celibacy then and there if it would have gotten me some ice.

I read the glossy 30 page brochure for the hotel services. It claimed there was an ice machine on the bottom floor — somewhere. When there's nothing else to do but shrug your shoulders, suck in your gut and get to it, that's what you do. I hobbled, hopped to the elevator and rode it down the 300 floors to the lobby. Directly in front of me was a sign that said "Ice/*hielo*." There was a fancy machine that didn't work and a deep freezer full of two kilo bags. On the way back, I was glad I didn't have to take that vow.

"Mexico" Mike hobbled back and finally saw a Yankee doctor in Mission ER. He shouldn't have been so pig-headed. Now he has a foot to match.

112

Taxi Drivers

Sunday, June 9, 1991

I've given up trying to understand anything. The fabric of Life is so intricately intertwined, so mysteriously woven that I just try to accept what comes and learn from it. Since my ignorance exceeds only my vanity, I get a lot of chances to learn.

If my brand-new used VW hadn't developed a mysterious malady I wouldn't have flown on my last trip. If I hadn't sprained my ankle, I wouldn't have taken so many taxis. If I hadn't talked to so many taxi drivers (*taxistas*), I wouldn't have learned what I did.

I always ask, "How's tourism this year?"

"Oh it is down, senor. This is not the season (*la temporada*)."

"I know. But compare it to last year. Are there fewer tourists this May than last May?"

"May was not the season last year either. The season is November to March."

"Ok, how about last November? Was it down from last year?"

"Si, there are many more tourists during November."

Last year was a disaster for tourism. I've asked the same questions for three years. I've gotten the same answers for three years. If you ask the same questions three years from now, you'll get the same answers, trust me.

Ask a New Orleans or New York cabby and he'll give you statistics and opinions you could base an article on. Many lazy travel writers do. The Mexican cabby doesn't have much use for statistics, or the past. It's now that counts. It's the next season, when everything will be better that counts.

In Acapulco, I've gone to the same laundromat, *lavandería* for three years. My memory wasn't very good when I had all my brain cells, so it's pretty shot now. I don't remember the name, but I know it's downtown, *centro*.

I flag down a cab, carrying three plastic sacks with socks hanging from the sides.

"Do you know a lavandería in the centro?"

They always smile. "Si, señor. I know a good one."

They always take me to one above town. I go in, though I know the place is a dry cleaner (*tintoria*), that sends laundry out. It takes 3 days. While I'm getting the name of the *lavandería* (Vic) where they send it, the taxista comes in for directions. Everybody smiles. I and my dirty socks pile back in. I thought this was a ploy to overcharge me, but the drivers agree to a fare and have never charged me extra for waiting, or driving a couple of miles more. I learned than a roundtrip fare is cheaper than two one-ways. A lawyer taught me that. He was also a taxista. Times are tough.

Twelve hours. That's what the

113

average taxi driver works, from Cancún to Acapulco. He makes three to five times minimum wage, which is about $4.00 a day. Most don't own their own cabs, but aspire to. Most don't have insurance. Most are honest. Many are good drivers. Some are just lucky.

In Cancún, a veteran Time-Life correspondent and I learned about human relations. A young kid picked us up. He was unfriendly from the beginning. My foot hurt. I wasn't too friendly myself. Then he began racing another driver down the main drag. The speedometer hit 90 KM when he won. He slowed to a sedate 60 KM. The speed limit was 30 KM.

I asked him to slow down. He sped up. He turned the radio up — loud. I suggested he turn it down. He snapped it off and sped up. My friend, who had been around, was white

We all have bad days. We all have egos. He'd proved he had a pretty good sized one. So had I. We were both losing. We'd all die if we kept competing. I looked around his car. It was spic-and-span. The dash was oiled; the mats were jet black and the seat was spotless. He had a dustrag in the ashtray.

The sun was gliding into the Caribbean to our left. A peaceful pink glow was rolling over the horizon. I looked past him to see it. He turned to look too.

"¡Qué magnifico!," I said.

"Si."

"Tranquilo." (Tranquil, peaceful.)

"Si. Ya lo creo." (You bet.)

We both stared in silence. He eased off the accelerator.

"Your car is very clean."

A hint of a smile came to his eyes.

"You must be very proud of it. It is the cleanest taxi I have ever seen."

"Gracias."

We slowed down to the speed limit. We made the rest of the trip in silence, all of us enjoying the tranquility of nature that can soothe us all when we get our egos out of the way and let God do His work.

Given the choice, I'd rather make a friend than a point. We always have the choice.

§§§§§§§§§§§§§§§§§§§§§§§§

"Mexico" Mike is too much of a grump to keep any friends, but we let him dream on. He spends most of his waking hours dreaming about writing Sanborn's Travelog and telling people where to go.

114

Mineral Water

After a wild taxi ride, I always get thirsty. Of course, quenching one's thirst can be easy or hard, depending on what one is willing to settle for. I reckon you know which of the two ways I choose.

Oh, most of you have read about the great beers that Mexico makes. There used to be hundreds of little breweries across the country that produced regional brews. Just like in the United States, they have folded, merged or dried up, so that now there are probably fewer than a dozen brands today.

Well, I'd like to think that I did my part to aid their demise, since I stopped imbibing them awhile back, but it probably would have happened anyway. I did get a few sobbing letters from brewmasters asking me why I'd jilted them.

One door never shuts, but another opens. I discovered "*refrescos*" (soft drinks). Those of you who only order "Coke™" or "Pepsi™" are missing the boat. That's okay, your soda-jerk captain is here to get you on the right course.

While there are number of small bottlers that make local soft drinks, the first choice of most tourists is "*agua mineral*" or mineral water. Many folks order this with their meals when they don't want something sweet. That's fine. What they don't realize is that it can be so much more.

There's a wide variety in mineral waters. Some of them have minerals and some of them don't. You already know that Mexicans are looser with their definitions of things. Sometimes "*agua mineral*" is merely "*agua purificada*" (purified water). Up north here, we're used to getting "Topo Chico™" when we order "agua mineral". This is fine for what it is, but it ain't mineral water.

"Peñafiel™" brand typifies what a mineral water should be. Look at the side of the bottle. It contains potassium, calcium carbonate, silicon, magnesium, a bunch of other stuff and best of all, lithium. Yep, the wonder drug of the 60's. Lithium was used to treat depression. While the amounts in a bottle of mineral water is pretty small, I think that's one of the reasons that some of us are bothered by almost nothing while we're in Mexico. I personally consume at least a six-pack a day. Old habits die hard.

"Peñafiel™" comes in "*sabores*" (flavors) for those who want their daily dosage of mellowness. You can order "*fresa*" (strawberry), "*naranja*" (orange), "*limón*" (lime) and others.

The best mineral waters come from the area around Tehuacán, in the state of Puebla, but there are bottling plants around the country. Some of the best brands are "Etiqueta Azul™", "Tehuacán™" "Peñafiel™"

115

Of course, once you develop a taste for a specific brand of "*agua mineral*", you won't be able to find it. Really. There's an unwritten law in Mexico that whatever you truly want you cannot get without a lot of hassle.

Part of the problem is that "*peñafiel*" or "*tehuacán*" are used generically - just like we use "coke" when we mean any kind of soft drink. Mexicans are far less brand conscious than we are. The last time I got into a fight with a bartender was in Huatulco, Oaxaca, over on the Pacific coast.

I asked for a "*Peñafiel*™" or a "*Tehuacán*™". He handed me a bottle of distilled water — the kind that you buy in liter-sized plastic jugs. Then he took my beads. (They don't use money at Club Med. In a Neanderthal reversal, they substitute beads. Different colors denote different denominations. I never figured out how many reds equaled a blue etc.).

I informed him (politely, as I always do), that **distilled** water was not **mineral** water. He informed me that in France it was. I suggested that he return to France. I even offered to help send him on his way. He came across the bar. Lucky for him that six of my friends held me back.

Though you usually won't have quite such a problem, you'll find that your average waiter will serve whatever brand he has on hand when you ask for a "Tehuacán". You can ask for "*Un agua mineral, por favor, la marca Tehuacán*™", (A mineral water, please, the brand

called Tehuacan.), but it won't do much good.

Why, then did I lead you down this primrose path only to snare you on the horns of a dilemma? Is it because I like mixed metaphors? No. Once you know what you want, you can try different ways to get it. You'll find yourself getting to know waiters (even if you don't speak Spanish) better than before. You'll have a chance to interact with them on a personal level. They'll be amazed that you know the difference in the brands, since most of them don't. You can explain it to them by showing the side of the bottle, which lists the "*minerales*" (minerals) in the brand.

The waiters will think it's pretty neat that a dumb gringo knows and appreciates something about his country that he took for granted. You'll leave a good impression. You'll be more mellow when you get your lithium fix. I don't think this is habit-forming but I brought this to the attention of the Great Zamba, who has moved on to editorship of the *Mexico City News*. Last time I was there, EVERYBODY was guzzling *Peñafiel*. They were all pretty mellow, too.

It may be the only time that knowing me has made anyone mellow. I try not to let that sort of thing get out of hand.

§§§§§§§§§§§§§§§§§§§§§

"Mexico" Mike has always drunk a lot. These days he can drink a lot without getting a lot drunk. He encourages tourists to try local soft drinks in their car trips through

Tequila, Mezcal, & Pulque

Sunday, June 23, 1991

Well, folks, it's birthday time! This column is a year old this week. That's right, you've been blessed (cursed) with fifty-two weeks worth of offbeat and off-the-wall information about Mexico from me. I don't know if anyone is any more well-informed, or well-traveled, but I've learned a lot. Now this column not only graces the pages of the *Monitor*, but the *Mexico City News* as well.

We've been on roads that don't go anywhere; played chicken with semi-trucks; met expatriates; eaten our way down the Gulf coast; and had heard some tall tales. I really appreciate all of you who've told me you read what I write. I hope it's not because you've nothing better to do, so I'll keep it up another year, with your permission.

I always like to clear up confusion; particularly if I didn't start it in the first place. I'm probably the first (ok, the second) to admit when I don't know anything. The advantage of that is I get to learn from a lot of folks.

Tequila, pulque and mezcal have always interested me. Alas, they used to interest me too much. Then my interest was dependant on how much money I had in my jeans.

Before I met Jo Liston of "Go With Jo" tours out of Harlingen I thought they were just different strengths of the same thing. She told me I was wrong. While she doesn't spend time testing tequila etc. she does know more about Mexico than I do. Since her competitor, Ed Gill who operates Sanborn's Viva Tours, was my first expert source on Mexico, I'm really lucky to know both. It was Jo, though, who got me interested in reading about magueys.

Then I met two more Mexicophiles, George Gause and Virginia Haney, who helped me with my source for my limited knowledge of the three Mexican drinks. I'm indebted to Virginia Bottorff de Barrios, editor of the Minutiae Mexicana book, "*a guide to Tequila, Mezcal and Pulque*". The series is a great place to get an overview of Mexican things.

Pulque comes from the maguey, Agave atrovirens. It's a big plant, and grows in a small area in the cold central highlands of central Mexico. It doesn't like rain. There are six or eight varieties. Tequila comes from the Agave tequiliana and it grows mainly in a small area around Guadalajara called Tequila, Jalisco. It has a bluish hue. Mezcal likes lower, warmer, wetter lands and grows on the coasts, but not in the tropical areas, although it pops up around Torreón and Durango and San Luis Potosí, so I guess it's not more democratic.

In short, mezcal is a hard liquor, artificially fermented. Tequila is a specific type of mezcal. Pulque is a product of natural fermentation and is ready in 24 hours. All come from some species of maguey.

A place that sells pulque exclusively is called a *pulquería*. It's a pretty low-class barroom. If you read Malcolm Lowry's classic novel, *"Under the Volcano"*, then you know what a pulquería is like. The main character had sunk to the depths of degradation. His last stop on the road to Hell was a pulquería.

Tradition holds that a pulquería floor should be sawdust, partly because another tradition calls for spilling some on the ground to quench Mother Nature's thirst. I've visited a few, but it's not for the timid. Strangers aren't encouraged. Women, are even less popular. Some pulquerías have a side window to serve women.

Pulque was probably around at the time of Christ. The *Aztecas* called the plant it came from *metl*. They called all maquey plants *metl*. As you can see, the lack of specification that plagues devotees of mineral water started long ago. The drink from the *metl* was *itac octli*. "White wine" will do as a translation. The Indians gave it another name when it went sour — *octli poliuhqui*. The Spaniards didn't pay attention and confused the name of the good stuff with the bad stuff. They called it *pulque*. They were probably drunk when writing. So, if you don't translate well, you're in historic, if not good, company. I figure the Indians enjoyed laughing at the "dumb Spaniards."

"Minutia" mentions a legend that pulque was originated by the Otomies, early settlers of Mexico, "... a group of ne'er do well, semi-nude barbarians who ate their meat raw and drank their liquor ("juice of the maguey") neat, in large quantities." Sounds like they've been reading my mail.

The Aztecs reserved pulque to priests, old people and nursing mothers. It was supposed to have special nutritional qualities.

Drunkenness was a real no-no. Your first drunk in Aztec times was your last. No foolin' The sentence for public intoxication was death. If you were a priest, though, you got a second chance after having your head shaved and sitting in the public square in humiliation. Your second wing-ding would fling you to your ancestors, though.

It was used by priests to heighten enthusiasm for sacrifices. It was also given to the victims. I guess it was to get them in the mood. Either way the stuff could kill you. On the "Day of the Dead", everybody consumes it in the graveyard.

The history is quite complex so if this was just enough to wet your thirst, you'll find a lot more to learn.

$$\$$$

"Mexico" Mike got thirsty while writing this and his handwriting became unintelligible. We hope he'll be back next week, but we don't know what he's got on (or in) his little mind.

118

Huatulco — The All-Inclusive Side

Sunday, June 30, 1991

Progress is a two-edged sword. It slices the bondage of poverty for many. It rips the fabric of memories for others. For some the bays of Huatulco have always been a special place. For many, those bays were unknown until 1988. For them the bays will be Mexico. They represent something good and unique about a land that I love; much that is unsettling. But, as a journalist, I must offer a fair report with my own biases clearly defined. I'm not the world's greatest judge of anything. I'm just a guy with an opinion.

The first time I saw Huatulco, it didn't exist. Santa Cruz existed, a fishing village, off Hwy 200 between the oil port of Salina Cruz and the bohemian mecca of Pto. Angel. All of these spots are in the state of Oaxaca. I was in a state of flux.

1984 — I was on my way to Pto. Escondido. I thought I was on my way to Acapulco. I was a burnout: a scared little guy with a tenuous grip on reality. Both Huatulco and I were in the planning stages then. Neither of us is what we were then; we're both what we have always been.

1985 — Overhead in the dirt-floor disco in Pto. Escondido: "You take the second-class bus. Tell the driver you want to get off at Santa Cruz. He'll stop at this dirt road. You get out. Hike a couple of miles. There's not much town, but you can buy warm beer, lobster and lots of fish. Great diving. Clear water. Schools of fish, unafraid. It's a trek, but man, it's worth it. You can hitch a ride with a fisherman going back to the highway. Man, the people who live there are the greatest. They're what Mexico is all about."

1991 — A group deplanes at the Huatulco Intl. Airport. We board an air-conditioned tour bus. A natty conductor offers us drinks from a styrofoam ice-bucket.

"I am sorry," he says in Oxford English, "we have only Diet Pepsi™ and regular Coke™. Our beers are Carta Blanca, Superior and Tecate."

Naturally, they didn't have Peñafiel.

We are given a "tour" of the 8, 9, 10 bays of Huatulco via a VCR and 25" TV. It's slick. Overhead shots of the bays, with a hawk's shadow rushing ahead. A perfect-bodied god and his goddess check into their tasteful suite in a high-rise hotel. Later, while other gods/goddesses fry on the perfect beaches, more of their tribe fish for the big ones, play volleyball in the pristine pool or doze.

Night comes to videolandia. The tribe attends a "Mexican Fiesta". Everybody smiles, including the waiters and waitresses. The close is tasteful, concentrating on the beauty of the area; the concern for the environment. That's the most that most of these people will see of the Bays of Huatulco.

We're put up in the **Royal Maeva**

119

(958-10000) — an all-inclusive resort. Everyone who greets us is upbeat, neat and shapely. Of course they are, that's their job. We are tired, grumpy and grubby, or at least I am. They are nice to us. They hand us our information packets and plastic keys. They brand us by snapping I.D. bracelets on our wrists. One lady said it reminded her of a concentration camp. I think of a prison, or a hospital. I rebel. The nice people are stunned. No one else has the bad manners to object. They put one around the pen that dangles from my neck. (Hey, I lose 'em otherwise.) All is smiles again.

"All-inclusive" means you pay one price for your vacation. With your room, meals, practically unlimited drinks (including mineral water), activities and social events are included. It's great for those who want to budget themselves. It's terrible for those who want to experiment. Therein lies the yin and the yang. Whether it is "good" or "bad" depends on what kind of person you are. I'm just ugly, so I don't count.

Norteamericano, Mexican & European families go for 'em, too. One lady described it as "summer camp for adults." There are activities for the kids, for you and wifey and the pressure of deciding what to do or where to go is gone. You can really enjoy your vacation.

Most people who go to these places never escape. They never know Mexico. They may be in Huatulco, but they could be in Peoria or Toluca with a beach and nicer weather. But, hey, that's what they want.

Advertising agency marketing research told the Mexican government this is what you and I want. Maybe I'm just out of step. Anyone who marched with me in the Bobcat band will attest to that. I was a band bench-warmer. My drummer is on another planet. I'll tell you about these places because they may be OK for you. You should also be aware of them, because many people who say, "I've been to Mexico," haven't. It's not their fault. They didn't want to go to Mexico. They wanted to go to a resort.

Next week, we'll escape, become ensnared in Club Med; narrowly miss being Med-ized (like lobotomized), and talk to some real folks in Santa Cruz. There are inexpensive hotels and "the people are (still) the greatest."

§§§§§§§§§§§§§§§§§§§§§

"Mexico" Mike has unreasonable fears that stem from his dark and disreputable past. We think he's lucky that any hotel above one star even lets him check in. They do count the towels and sheets before he leaves, though.

Huatulco — The Real People Side

Sunday, July 7, 1991

It's people that make Mexico attractive. Even Huatulco, Oaxaca has people who make those like me keep coming back. Sure, it has gorgeous beaches and fancy hotels and nightlife — all those things that bring the other breed of tourist, God bless 'em. Sometimes those of us who think we know something get a little too arrogant and think we're the only tourists who count. For the Mexican who works with tourists, we are the oddballs. He has to learn to deal with all of us.

Huatulco is really three places: Santa Cruz, Huatulco, & La Crucesita. Huatulco is the mega-resort. Santa Cruz is where the first hotel (**Posada Binniguenda #5 Paseo Benito Juarez, Santa Cruz,** PH: (958) 4-0077, (D.F. (5) 687-8000) and the market were built. La Crucesita is the town where you'll find guys like me, and others who want inexpensive eats and sheets. I met Sr. Antonio Morales B. in the market. He opened my eyes and my mind.

When you enter the market, you'll be assaulted by English. Signs are in English; vendors call you, "My friend." In many ways you are. Tourism brings dollars. Dollars buy food, medicine, a chance to change.

Sr. Morales owns a "shop" in the market. It's a stall, really. Everything is neat, orderly, clean. He sells every kind of trinket or "typical" item you can imagine in an 8 by 12 area. I'm not a shopper. I hate to shop — anywhere. I was there because it beat hanging around the Club Med.

Briefly, my Club Med experience taught me that there are lots of people in the world who like being told what to do. It makes them feel secure. I'd rather feel insecure. After I fought with the bartender about "agua mineral", I ran screaming away, ripping the plastic ID bracelet from my wrist. Everybody was glad to see me go.

Sr. Morales is dignified. He's a salesman, but not a hustler. I said something about "the way things used to be."

"My friend, you obviously know Mexico, but you do not know Mexicans."

He said it in such a way that I couldn't take offence.

"Yes, the area was beautiful before the resort. The people who lived here had a very pretty place. They also had little else. Now, they have a hospital, doctors and schools for their children."

"But didn't one of your presidents say that he didn't want Mexico to become a nation of busboys and waiters?"

"True, some make only the minimum wage and some will carry bags. But the bright ones will see that there is a future, that they can become something besides a fisherman. They will get the education, or their children will."

121

"Aren't the multinational corporations taking all the money?"

He laughed, softly. "Come," he said. He took my hand and led me to the other side of the market, across the pink cobblestone street, down the side of the marina. We came to an area that was not so neat, that had real dirt and real tin-roofed lean-tos. Standing behind a real fire inverted black-domed portable Mexican wok that is "real" Mexico, was Doña María. She had a "lagarto"-wrinkled face, and when she smiled, a couple of teeth missed the grand opening. Groups of workers from around the area, were eating out of red-green-blue plastic plates on a long wooden plank that served as a table. They perched on stools — some wooden, some barroom rejects. The open air was thick with the homey smell of hot tortillas, spiced beef and the snapping pork frying on the grill.

"My friend, this woman would be cleaning fish for less per week than she makes per day here. She is a businesswoman. She would not have this opportunity if it weren't for the "other" Mexico."

He pointed at a young boy of ten. He sat at a corner stool, oblivious to his surroundings. Before him lay a book — a real book, not a comic, which you see so often.

"He's learned to read. Tomorrow he will be a manager or doctor. Maybe today he may have to be a busboy, or waiter, but he has many tomorrows now."

I walked away, feeling pensive. We who live with running water, soft beds and three squares find it easy to tell others how they should live. But would we want to follow our own advice? Hell, instead of a waiter, the kid might grow up to be a writer. Then he could tell the true story. Until then, I'll just do the best I can, with my limited view.

Here are some hotels that won't gobble up your wallet. All are $25-$45 per couple. **Busanni** — Calle Carrisal, Lote 11, Manzana 10, **La Crucesita,** PH: no — 12 rooms. Ceiling fans. **Casa Robert** — Calle 11, Lote 4, Sec. E, **Santa Cruz,** PH: no — Homey place off main drag (B. Juarez) at end (for now) of hotel district. 5 rooms, ceiling fans, flush against a hill, surrounded by lush vegetation. A small, family-run place, it typifies the entrepreneurial spirit. It's not for everybody, but if you want to feel like you're with a family, check it out. **Grifer** — Av. Guamuchi, corner Carrizal, **La Crucesita,** PH: 7-0048 — 20 rooms, ceiling fans. **La Casita** — Chacah Manzana #14, Lote 3, **La Crucesita,** PH: no — 4 rooms. A/C, some with view. Very pleasant, homey atmosphere. TOURISM INFO — Ph: 4-0030, 4-0262, 4-0246, ext 124.

Index

A

AAA 43 - 44, 59, 61
  AMERICAN AUTOMOBILE
ASSOCIATION   43
Agave Atrovirens   117
Agua Mineral   115 - 116, 121
All-inclusive   119 - 120
Aqueducts 61
Arizona
  Cottonwood, AZ 66
  Nogales, AZ   1, 109
Art   3 - 4, 65 - 66
Aztec Custom RV Tours   54
Aztecs   3, 47, 79, 81, 118

B

Babcock, Jim   56
Baja California, Sur
  Cabo San Lucas, BCS 72
Bandidos   81
Bardot, Brigitte   31
Beckham, Nancy, Paige   24
Buckman, Gene   99
Booze   19, 111
Botone   111
Burnout   119
Burton, Richard   84

C

Cabo San Lucas, BCS 72
Caliente 103
California
  Hollywood, CA   4, 24, 110 -
111
  Santa Barbara, CA   21
Cameras   19
Canaco   86
Cancn, Q. R.   28, 42, 51, 84, 106,
111, 114
Car   19, 49, 63, 70, 76, 114
Caravans   87
Caravans Mexico & Central
America   54
Carr, Peter J.   16
CB'S 19

Chamber of Commerce 86
Chiapas   2 - 3, 20, 47 - 49, 106
  Palenque, CHI   79, 106
  San Cristbal de las Casas, CHI
89, 106
Chihuahua
  Chihuahua   41 - 42, 55 - 56,
58
  Copper Canyon (Creel)   41 -
43, 54 - 56, 109
  San Juanito   55
  Sierra Madre Occidental
Mountains   41
Citizenship   19
Citrus   57, 107
Classic Period (300-900 AD)
105
Cleaver, Paul Nunn   23
Coahuila
  Saltillo 41, 75, 84, 107
Coffins   75
Coldwell, Pedro Joaqun   81
Colima
  Manzanillo   87, 93 - 94
Colonial Mexico   54
Computers 19
Conrad, Joseph 41
Contraloria   19
Contreras, Eric   21
  Eric the Heroic   33, 46
Cosmic Cowboy   79

D

D.F.   20, 32, 90, 121
Dal, Salvador 105
Dan's Sanborn Story   70, 101
Dangerous 99
de Alonzo, Hctor Maricruz   76
de Barrios, Virginia Bottorff 117
Death   33 - 34, 79, 83
Demonstrate   19
Devil's Backbone   63
Da de Comercio y el Turista   86
Dios 35

Distrito Federal
  Mexico City, DF   4, 8, 20,
21, 27, 32, 44, 48, 51, 57, 90, 99 -
100, 115 - 116
Dos Cuadras   104
Driving   1 - 3, 5 - 8, 15, 17, 26,
31 - 32, 37, 41, 43 - 44, 67 - 69,
90, 93, 105, 107, 109, 113
Driving Different   2, 51
Drugs   19, 86
Durango
  Durango   43, 109 - 110, 117,
121 - 122
  Torren   41, 117

E

Egos   114
El Hombre Preparado 79
Eleanor   72 - 73
Embalm   71, 101
Escobedo, Manuel   21
Exorcise 35

F

Farmacia 86
Fat Man, Little Boy 110
Fear 2, 15, 32, 57, 81, 120
Festivals 33, 118
  Dates   33
  Death   33 - 34, 79, 83
  Feast of San Bartolo   33
  fireworks 33
  Janitzio, MICH 33
  Oaxaca   2 - 3, 17, 20 - 23, 25,
27, 33 - 34, 47, 87, 116, 119, 121
  skulls   33
  The Day of the Dead 33
Fields, W. C. 65
Fireplaces   42, 77
Fishing/Hunting   7
Food 7, 9 - 10, 14, 19, 33, 41 -
42, 46, 50 - 51, 57, 61, 66, 100,
121
Ford 6, 87, 97 - 98
Fro 103

Frustrations   112
Furniture 45, 61, 85, 109

G

Galera Vallarta   82
Gamboa, Jorge   27
Gaos, Carlos Camacho   27
Garca, Rolando   27
Gas
  Diesel   2, 17
  Extra   1, 3, 7, 13, 18, 27,
32, 47
  Gasolinera   90
  Magna Sin 32
  Pemex   8, 12 - 14, 43 - 44,
47 - 48, 55, 90, 92
  Unleaded Gas   1, 17, 21, 32,
37, 47 - 48, 85
Gause, George   117
Ghosts   11, 78 - 79, 99
Gill, Ed 57, 117
God   5, 35 - 36, 67, 73, 114
Gold Zone 82
Good, The Bad and the Ugly,
The   69
Grandma   101 - 102
Grazer, Arlyne 23
Green Angels   2, 17, 27, 31, 70
Gulf Coast   13, 27, 32, 47, 87,
93, 105, 117
Guns 20

H

Ham Radios   20
Haney, Virginia   1170
Hemingway 109
Heroism   21
Hielera   111
Highways
  #16 42
  #175 21
  #180 5, 7, 13, 27, 31 - 32, 47
  #200 25

124

#200 25
#35 84
#40 41, 43
#45 41
#54 32, 67, 84
#57 43, 67, 75, 84
#80 84
#85 35, 59, 70, 97, 99, 107
#97 3
   Guadalajara-Tepic 84
Homlberg, Bill 87
Hotels 11, 29, 45, 53
   Bisbee, AZ 56
   Cabo San Lucas, BCS 5
   Cd. Victoria, TAMPS 57, 62
   Copper Canyon (Creel), CHIH 41, 55
   Durango, DGO 1 - 2
   Guadalajara, JAL 84 - 85
   Huatulco, OAX 116, 119 - 122
   La Pesca, TAMPS 5, 84
   Matehuala, SLP 71
   Mazatln, NAY 37, 39, 65
   Nautla, VER 27
   Oaxaca, OAX 34, 51, 57 - 58
   Pochutla, OAX 21
   Pto. Angel, OAX 25
   Pto. Escondido, OAX 23
   Pto. Vallarta, JAL 45 - 46, 84 - 85, 27
   Real de Catorce, SLP 78
   San Fernando, TAMPS 3 - 5
   Santa Cruz, OAX 121
   Tampico, TAMPS 9 - 12, 47 - 50, 101, 105
   Tecolutla, VER 31
   Tuxpan, VER 30
   Zacatecas, ZAC 84 - 85
Huatulco, Oax. 25, 116, 119 - 121
   Hotels 116, 120 - 122
Huichol 64
Huichol Center 65 - 66
Huston, John 84

I

Ice 111 - 112

Insurance 17
Isla Mujeres, Q. Roo 111

J

Jacobs, Bob & Pat 93
Jacuzzi 29, 45, 53, 64, 72, 76, 84, 94, 105
Jails 57
Jalisco
   Lagos de Moreno, JAL 84, 93
   Pto. Vallarta, JAL 53, 81 - 82, 84 - 85
   Tequila, JAL 117
James, Edward 105R Jefe 19
Josephina 79

K

Keller, Dr. Barry 21
Kids 19, 31, 88
King's Mines 108
Kowalski, Henry 3, 47
Krishnamurti, J. 66

L

La Crucesita, Oax. 121 - 122
Leather 98, 105
Left turn signal 2, 17
Life in Mexico 19
Liga Mexicana de Radio Experimentadores 19
Liquado 9, 49
Liquor 20, 117 - 118
Liston, Jo 117
Lithium 115 - 116
Living in Mexico 94
Lone Woman 89
Lpez, Suzanne & Mateo 25
Los Altares 107
Lowry, Malcom 33, 117
   Under the Volcano 33, 118

M

Mailer, Norman 78
Mark 78 - 79
Mechanic 36, 63, 87, 97 - 98, 110
Mennonites 41 - 42, 57 - 58, 105

125

Mctl 118
Mexican Insurance 1, 17, 19, 37
Mexican Tourism Dept.   2
Mexicanism   55, 57
Mexico East Coast, Belize and Guatemala RV   54
Mezcal   117
Michoacn
Janitzio 33
Lago Ptzcuaro   33
Mineral Water 115 - 116, 118, 120
Minimum Wage 114, 121
Minutiae Mexicana 117
miracle 35 - 36, 57 - 59, 66, 105
Missionaries 16, 35
Mordida 3, 27
Morelos
Cuernavaca, MOR   78
Mountain Kingdom   107
Mountains 5, 37, 41, 51, 57, 55, 75 - 76, 81 - 82, 107, 110
Cerro de la Bufa   108
Murray, Steve 7

N

Napoleonic Code   17
Nayarit
La Laguna de Santa Mara del Oro, NAY 84
Santiago Ixcuintla, NAY 64 - 65
New Mexico
Santa Fe, NM   109
Night Driving   2, 11, 17, 22, 33 - 34, 36, 47 - 48, 53 - 54, 57 - 58, 73, 79, 102, 105, 107 - 108, 119, 121
Night of the Iguana 84
Nuevo Len
Aramberri, NL 107
China, NL 107
Monterrey, NL 17, 41, 81, 84, 93, 95, 107
San Roberto Junction   84
Nuevo Vallarta 82

O

Oaxaca 2 - 3, 18 - 19, 21 - 23, 25, 27, 33 - 34, 47, 87, 116, 119, 121
Huatulco, OAX 25, 116, 119 - 121
Indians 33, 118
La Crucesita, OAX 121 - 122
Marinero Beach, OAX 23 - 24
Pochutla, OAX 21, 25
Pto. Angel, OAX   21, 25, 119
Pto. Escondido, OAX 21, 23, 79, 119
Santa Cruz, OAX   119 - 122
Oscar   83
Otomies 118
Owens, John Kinsey 41, 56

P

Padre Harold 35 - 36
Paige, Satchel 78
Pan American Highway   99
Pancho Villa   41
Patoski, Joe Nick   105
PB 103
Pemex   8, 12 - 14, 43 - 44, 47 - 48, 55, 90, 92
Prez Basanez, Jorge   29
Peters, Gene & Barbara   81
Pets 19
Picasso 105
Pinlocillo   61
Pinche 36
Planta Baja   103
Potholes 14 - 15, 32, 67 - 68
Prisoners 61, 93
Progress 72

Huatulco   119
Prove   19
Pto. Angel, Oax.   21, 25, 119
Pto. Escondido, Oax.   21, 23, 79, 119
Pulque   117 - 118
Pulquera 90 - 91, 118

Q

Quintana Roo
   Cancn   28, 42, 51, 84, 106, 111, 114
   Isla Mujeres   111

R

Ramos, Ing. Juan Arturo Lpez   34
Refi, John   23
Registro Federal de Vehculos 3
Restaurants
   Copper Canyon (Creel), CHIH 56
   Dallas, TX   24
   Naranjos, VER   14
   Oaxaca, OAX   34
   Pto. Vallarta, JAL   46
   Sinaloa   85
   Tampico, TAMPS 9 - 10, 50
Retirement   70, 94
Ro Panuco   13
Roads   2, 4 - 5, 15, 17, 27, 31, 33, 37, 41 - 42, 48, 55 - 56, 67, 74 - 75, 87 - 88, 93, 95, 99, 107, 117
Roadside Vendors   107
Romo, Lic. Gilberto Caldern   27
Ruz, Ventura   75
RV Park
   La Laguna de Santa Mara del Oro, NAY   84

S

Safety   2
Salinas, President   43, 90
San Luis Potos
   Cd. Valles, SLP   105
   Cedral, SLP   75
   Charcas, SLP   67
   Matehuala, SLP 43, 67, 71, 75, 84, 90
   Moctezuma, SLP 68
   Real de Catorce, SLP   67, 75 - 78, 107
   San Juan Sin Agua, SLP   35
   Tamazunchale, SLP   70, 97, 99
   Xilitla, SLP   107
Sanborn, Mr.   67, 70, 101
Santa Cruz, Oax.   70, 119 - 121
Servibars 23, 111
Shortcuts 67, 69
Sinaloa   41, 43
   Concordia 109
   Los Mochis   41, 55, 109
   Mazatln   3, 37 - 40, 65, 42 - 43, 109
   Topolobombo   56
Slick, Grace   24
Smokes   57, 61
Sonora
   lamos   109
Stephens, Roger   99
Stolen   17, 46
Stuff   19
Sugar Haciendas   61
Sunset   8, 24, 39, 47, 72 - 73, 76

T

Tabasco
   Villahermosa, TAB   88
Tamaulipas
   Cd. Miguel Alemn 86
   Cd. Victoria 57 - 58, 59, 61, 70, 105
   El Chorrito   59, 61
   Fishing   7
   La Pesca   5 - 7, 26, 105
   Nuevo Laredo 99
   Reynosa 3
   RV Parks   8
   San Fernando 3, 5, 32, 47
   Tampico 3, 7 - 10, 18, 27, 32, 47 - 51, 101, 105
taxidermista 101 - 102

taxista 113
Taylor, Liz 84
Tequila 117
Texans 81, 85 - 86, 95, 108
Texas
  Beaumont 99
  Bowie 99
  Brownsville 9, 47, 54, 57, 105
  Dallas 23 - 24, 41, 51
  Laredo 105
  McAllen 1 - 2, 5, 8 - 9, 14, 21, 26 - 27, 41, 47, 56 - 57, 70, 74, 84, 89, 93, 96, 101, 105
  Monthly Magazine 105
  Padre Island 31, 50, 84
  Roma 86
Thompson, Hunter 78
Time 4, 23 - 25, 37, 39, 51, 78, 113 - 114
Time-Life 114
Totonac 29, 105
Travel Alone 88 - 89
Travel Companion Exchange 89
Travelling Alone 89
Travelog 1, 4, 6, 8, 10, 12, 14, 20, 22, 25, 27 - 28, 30, 32, 34, 36 - 37, 42 - 43, 51, 54, 60, 64, 66, 68, 70 - 71, 77, 80, 83, 85, 87, 94 - 96, 100, 102, 107, 114, 116
Traven 36
Traven, B. 17, 19, 33
Treasure of the Sierra Madre, The 8, 67
Tripshare 8, 26, 32, 34, 88 - 89
tunnel 56, 75 - 77, 107
TV's 19

U

Under the Volcano 33, 118
Unleaded Gas 1, 17, 21, 32, 37, 47 - 48, 85
Unsafe 15, 43

V

Valadez, Susana Eger 64 - 65
Veracruz 7, 13, 27, 32, 47, 51, 102, 105
  Catemaco 20
  El Tajn 93, 105
  Gutirrez Zamora 31
  Naranjos 14, 27
  Ozuluma 14
  Papantla 105
  Poza Rica 105
  Tecolutla 31, 54
  Tuxpan 27 - 30, 32, 51, 94, 102
  Veracruz 105
Video Equipment 19
Volcanic Lake 106

W

Walker, Steve 10, 15
Wallace, Lucy 75
Witches 105 - 106

Y

Yelland, Norm 54, 87

Z

Zacatecas
  Zacatecas, ZAC 32, 69, 84 - 85, 103, 107
Zamba, Michael 21, 33, 90, 94, 116
Zanoni, Rita 82

If you liked this book of the infamous "Mexico" Mike's columns, reprinted from the Mexico City *News,* & the McAllen *Monitor,* use this handy-dandy form to order more. Send $6.95 (& $2.75 shipping & handling ($3.75 outside U.S.A.)) to: *Sanborn's, Dept Books-MM, P.O. Box 310, McAllen, TX 78502.*

Please send me _____ copies of the collected works of "Mexico" Mike's columns. I've enclosed $_____ in check or money order, payable to "TGP — Books", or charge my credit card (circle one) MASTERCARD or VISA Acct # _____, Expires, _____ .

Name on card, _____

Signature (required for credit card orders), _____

Ship to:

Name:_____

Street or PO Box:_____

City:_____ State:___ Zip:_____

Country:_____

Allow 4-6 weeks for delivery. Or drop into our McAllen office & pick one up.

If you liked this book of the infamous "Mexico" Mike's columns, reprinted from the Mexico City *News,* & the McAllen *Monitor.* use this handy-dandy form to order more. Send $6.95 (& $2.75 shipping & handling ($3.75 outside U.S.A.)) to: *Sanborn's, Dept Books-MM, P.O. Box 310, McAllen, TX 78502.*

Please send me _____ copies of the collected works of "Mexico" Mike's columns. I've enclosed $_____ in check or money order, payable to "TGP — Books", or charge my credit card (circle one) MASTERCARD or VISA Acct # _____, Expires, _____ .

Name on card, _____

Signature (required for credit card orders), _____

Ship to:

Name:_____

Street or PO Box:_____

City:_____ State:___ ZIP:_____

Country:_____

Allow 4-6 weeks for delivery. Or drop into our McAllen office & pick one up.

If you liked this book of the infamous "Mexico" Mike's columns, reprinted from the Mexico City *News*, & the McAllen *Monitor*, use this handy-dandy form to order more. Send $6.95 (& $2.75 shipping & handling ($3.75 outside U.S.A.)) to: *Sanborn's, Dept Books-MM, P.O. Box 310, McAllen, TX 78502.*

Please send me _____ copies of the collected works of "Mexico" Mike's columns. I've enclosed $_____ in check or money order, payable to "TGP — Books", or charge my credit card (circle one) MASTERCARD or VISA

Acct # _____, Expires, _____.

Name on card, _____

Signature (required for credit card orders), _____

Ship to:

Name: _____

Street or PO Box: _____

City: _____ State: ___ Zip: _____

Country: _____

CORRECTED PRICE IS $8.95 PLUS S&H

Allow 4-6 weeks for delivery. Or drop into our McAllen office & pick one up.

If you liked this book of the infamous "Mexico" Mike's columns, reprinted from the Mexico City *News*, & the McAllen *Monitor*. use this handy-dandy form to order more. Send $6.95 (& $2.75 shipping & handling ($3.75 outside U.S.A.)) to: *Sanborn's, Dept Books-MM, P.O. Box 310, McAllen, TX 78502.*

Please send me _____ copies of the collected works of "Mexico" Mike's columns. I've enclosed $_____ in check or money order, payable to "TGP — Books", or charge my credit card (circle one) MASTERCARD or VISA

Acct # _____, Expires, _____.

Name on card, _____

Signature (required for credit card orders), _____

Ship to:

Name: _____

Street or PO Box: _____

City: _____ State: ___ ZIP: _____

Country: _____

Allow 4-6 weeks for delivery. Or drop into our McAllen office & pick one up.